Series / Number 07-124

NEURAL NETWORKS

HERVÉ ABDI
The University of Texas at Dallas

DOMINIQUE VALENTIN
Université de Bourgogne à Dijon

BETTY EDELMAN
The University of Texas at Dallas

SAGE PUBLICATIONS
The International Professional Publi
Thousand Oaks   London   New Del

D1293075

For information:

SAGE Publications, Inc.
2455 Teller Road
Thousand Oaks, California 91320
E-mail: order@sagepub.com

SAGE Publications Ltd.
6 Bonhill Street
London EC2A 4PU
United Kingdom

SAGE Publications India Pvt. Ltd.
M-32 Market
Greater Kailash I
New Delhi 110 048 India

Printed in the United States of America

Library of Congress Cataloging-in-Publication Data

Abdi, Hervé.
   Neural networks / Hervé Abdi, Dominique Valentin, Betty Edelman.
     p. cm. — (Sage university papers series. Quantitative applications in the social sciences; 07-0124)
   Includes bibliographical references.
   ISBN 0-7619-1440-4
   1. Neural networks (Computer science). I. Valentin, Dominique.
II. Edelman, Betty. III. Title. IV. Series: Sage university papers series. Quantitative applications in the social sciences; 07-0124.
QA76.87.A325   1999
006.3′2—dc21   98-46918

This book is printed on acid-free paper.

99 00 01 02 03 04 05 7 6 5 4 3 2 1

Acquiring Editor:	C. Deborah Laughton
Editorial Assistant:	Eileen Carr
Production Editor:	Astrid Virding
Editorial Assistant:	Nevair Kabakian
Designer/Typesetter:	Hervé Abdi

When citing a university paper, please use the proper form. Remember to cite the Sage University Paper series title and incude the paper number. One of the following formats can be adapted (depending on the style manual used):

(1) ABDI, H., VALENTIN, D., and EDELMAN, B. (1999). *Neural Networks*. Sage University Papers Series on Quantitative Applications in the Social Sciences, 07-124. Thousand Oaks, CA: Sage.

OR

(2) Abdi, H., Valentin, D., & Edelman, B. (1999). *Neural networks* (Sage University Papers Series on Quantitative Application in the Social Sciences, series no. 07-124). Thousand Oaks, CA: Sage.

CONTENTS

SERIES EDITOR'S INTRODUCTION

Neural networks are quantitative models linking inputs and outputs adaptively in a learning process analogous to that used by the human brain. The networks consist of elementary units, labeled neurons, joined by a set of rules and weights. The units code characteristics, and they appear in layers, the first being the input layer and the last being the output layer. The data under analysis are processed through different layers, with learning taking place through alteration of the weights connecting the units. At the final iteration, the association between the input and output patterns is established. The example pursued to good expository effect in *Neural Networks* is face recognition patterns. In the simplest instance, Dr. Hervé Abdi and his colleagues, Dominique Valentin and Betty Edelman, develop a perceptron model that recognizes faces as "boy" or "girl." The input units consist of facial features (hair, eyes, nose, mouth, ears), coded as belonging to a "boy" or a "girl," and the output unit is coded 1 or 0, categorizing the face as "boy" or "girl." After three iterations, the perceptron could make correct classifications, at least when all the congruent features were present.

Improvement in classifications was possible because the connection weights between the input and output units were altered by means of a learning rule. The most widely known is the Widrow-Hoff learning rule, which directs attention to the input cells that are less error prone.

Besides the perceptron model, the authors explicate the linear autoassociative memory, the linear heteroassociative memory, and the backpropagation networks models. The models are presented in ascending order of complexity. In understanding neural networks, analogy is helpful. Besides similarities to the workings of the brain, the models have strong parallels to statistical procedures commonly used in the social sciences. The perceptron has a correspondence to discriminant analysis, linear autoassociative memory to principal component analysis, linear heteroassociative memory to multiple regression, and backpropagation to logistic regression. A grasp of these statistical analogies is a good aid to understanding what, for most social scientists, will be very new material. It is important to remember, however, that the neural network models are not equivalent to these statistical models. Neural network models come from adaptive, systematic search strategies applied to a particular sample. The empirical results are not intended to be parameter estimates of population values, based on a random sample and subject to the scrutiny of, say, the classical regression assumptions required for statistical inference.

Research on neutral networks has been going on for some time—for example, the perceptron was built in the 1950s. Interest declined from the 1960s until the 1980s, when it was renewed. Probably, according to the authors, this renewal of interest resulted from the spreading appreciation of error backpropagation, which could correct weights in the hidden layers. Currently, work in the area is vigorous, led by cognitive psychologists, statisticians, engineers, and mathematicians. The authors provide a useful bibliography in these different fields, as well as referencing the classic texts. Their own monograph provides a readable introduction to this dynamic, relatively new methodology of investigation.

—*Michael S. Lewis-Beck*
Series Editor

Notations

Symbol	Meaning	Page
a, $\mathbf{a}$, $\mathbf{b}$	activation scalar, vectors	5, 78, 76
$\mathbf{c}_\ell$, $\mathbf{C}$	RBF center vector, matrix	63, 64
$\cos(\widehat{\mathbf{x}}_k, \mathbf{x})$	cosine between $\widehat{\mathbf{x}}_k$ and $\mathbf{x}$	30
d, $\mathbf{d}$, $\mathbf{D}$	distance: scalar, vector, matrix	64
e, $\exp\{x\}$	$\approx 2.719\ldots$, exponential of $x = e^x$	63
e_k, $\mathbf{e}$, $\mathbf{E}$	error, error term vector, matrix	36, 37
$\widehat{e}_k$, $\widehat{\mathbf{e}}$	estimated error, vector	73, 75
f f', $\boldsymbol{f}$	function and derivative, vector function	74, 62
h_ℓ, $\mathbf{h}$	hidden activation, vector	73, 74
$\mathsf{H}\{x\}$	Heaviside or step function	5
i, I	an input cell, # of input cells	5
$\mathbf{I}$	Identity matrix	42
j, J	an output cell, # of ouput cells	8
$\mathcal{J}_k$, $\mathcal{J}$	an error function for pattern k, global	46, 20
k, K	a pattern, # of patterns	8
ℓ, L	a hidden cell or an eigenthing, # of	8, 41
logist, tanh	logistic, hyperbolic tangent	71
n, $[n]$	iteration #n, a matrix at iteration n	11
$s_{k,\ell}$, $\mathbf{s}$, $\mathbf{S}$	similarity: scalar, vector, matrix	64
t_j, $\mathbf{t}_k$, $\mathbf{T}$	target value: cell, pattern, set	10, 11
$\widehat{t}_j$, $\widehat{\mathbf{t}}_k$, $\widehat{\mathbf{T}}$	target estimate: cell, pattern, set	10, 48
$\text{trace}\{\mathbf{X}\}$	trace: sum of diagonal elements	37
$\mathbf{u}$, $\mathbf{v}$, $\mathbf{U}$, $\mathbf{V}$	eigen and singular vectors and matrices	42
$w_{i,j}$, $\mathbf{w}$, $\mathbf{W}$	weight to output layer: scalar, cell, set	8
$x_{i,k}$, $\mathbf{x}_k$, $\mathbf{X}$	input: element, vector, matrix	24
$\widehat{x}_i$, $\widehat{\mathbf{x}}_k$, $\widehat{\mathbf{X}}$	input estimate: element, vector, matrix	29, 48
$z_{i,\ell}$, $\mathbf{z}$, $\mathbf{Z}$	weight to hidden layer: scalar, cell, set	69
γ, η	"gamma, eta" learning constants	25, 10
δ, $\boldsymbol{\delta}$	nonlinear error signal: element, vector	73
δ_ℓ, $\boldsymbol{\Delta}$, λ_ℓ, $\boldsymbol{\Lambda}$	"delta," "lambda"; singular and eigenvalues	42, 41
Δ_w, $\boldsymbol{\Delta}_{\mathbf{W}}$	change to make, matrix of	10, 11
ϑ	"theta" threshold	5
ϱ, σ^2	"rho," "sigma," Gaussian function, variance	63
$\sum$, $\circledast$	Summation sign, Hadamar product	5, 64
ϕ	"phi" (RBF basis functions)	62
$\boldsymbol{\Phi}_{[n]}$	"Phi" eigenvalues matrix at time $[n]$	43
∇, $\frac{\partial f}{\partial x}$	gradient, partial derivative	45
$\mathbf{X}^T$, $\mathbf{X}^{-1}$, $\mathbf{X}^+$	transpose, inverse, pseudo-inverse of $\mathbf{X}$	8, 42, 59
$\|\mathbf{x}\|$	norm or length of $\mathbf{x}$	30

NEURAL NETWORKS

HERVÉ ABDI
The University of Texas at Dallas

DOMINIQUE VALENTIN
Université de Bourgogne à Dijon

BETTY EDELMAN
The University of Texas at Dallas

1. INTRODUCTION

1.1 What Are Neural Networks?

Neural networks are adaptive statistical models based on an analogy with the structure of the brain. They are *adaptive* in that they can learn to estimate the parameters of some population using a small number of exemplars (one or a few) at a time. They do not differ *essentially* from standard statistical models. For example, one can find neural network architectures akin to discriminant analysis, principal component analysis, logistic regression, and other techniques. In fact, the same mathematical tools can be used to analyze standard statistical models and neural networks. Neural networks are used as *statistical tools* in a variety of fields, including psychology, statistics, engineering, econometrics, and even physics. They are used also as *models* of cognitive processes by neuro- and cognitive scientists.

Basically, neural networks are built from simple units, sometimes called *neurons* by analogy. These units are interlinked by a set of weighted connections. Learning is usually accomplished by modification of the connection weights. Each unit codes or corresponds to a feature or a characteristic of a pattern that we want to analyze or that we want to use as a predictor. The units are organized in layers.

Thanks are due to Jay Dowling, Richard Golden, Patrick Lemaire, Ben Murdock, Mette Posamentier, Roger Ratcliff, Marsha Smith, John Vokey, and some other (anonymous) reviewers for comments on previous versions of this book. Thanks also to Pascal Périchon for his help in designing the LaTeX style for this volume.

In this introductory book, we will only present feedforward neural networks. These networks usually have several layers. The first layer is called the *input* layer, the last one the *output* layer. The intermediate layers (if any) are called the *hidden* layers. The information to be analyzed is fed to the neurons of the first layer and then propagated to the neurons of the second layer for further processing. The result of this processing is then propagated to the next layer and so on until the last layer. Each unit receives some information from other units (or from the external world through some devices) and processes this information, which will be converted into the output of the unit.

The goal of the network is to learn, or to discover, some association between input and output patterns. This learning process is achieved through the modification of the connection weights between units. In statistical terms, this is equivalent to interpreting the value of the connections between units as parameters (e.g., like the values of a and b in the regression equation $\widehat{y} = a + bx$) to be estimated. The learning process specifies the "algorithm" used to estimate the parameters.

1.2 Overview of This Book

In this book, we present some of the basic models. Each model is presented along with an example, which can be computed by hand or with a simple calculator. Because neural network models have strong relationships with statistical models, we also discuss the interpretation of neural networks as statistical models in each chapter. The models presented are the following.

- *The perceptron* (Chapter 2), even though not a very powerful model, is easy to analyze and allows for a straightforward introduction of important concepts such as the Widrow-Hoff learning rule and state space. It is shown to be akin to discriminant analysis.

- *The linear autoassociative memory* (Chapter 3) is included to show some of the key properties of neural networks. Hebbian learning is introduced in this chapter and contrasted with Widrow-Hoff learning. The opposition between supervised and unsupervised learning is also discussed. The autoassociative memory is shown to be closely related to principal component analysis.

- *The linear heteroassociative memory* (Chapter 4) is a generalization of the perceptron and corresponds to multiple linear regression. It allows for a smooth transition to error backpropagation networks and also for the introduction of the generalized inverse. The radial basis function, which handles nonlinear associations, is introduced as a variation of this type of memory.

- *Backpropagation networks* (Chapter 5) are the most well known and most frequently used neural networks. They can be interpreted as "universal approximators" and are used to estimate the values of parameters via a gradient descent algorithm in problems equivalent to nonlinear regression.

(Some other models, such as Anderson's BSB, Kosko's BAM, Hopfield networks, Kohonen's LVQ, and Grossberg's ART, are reserved for another volume in the series.)

2. THE PERCEPTRON

2.1 Overview

Constructed in the 1950s by Rosenblatt (1961), the perceptron can be considered as the first neural network capable of learning. An equivalent model called the *Adaline* was independently developed within a signal processing framework by Widrow around the same time. As its name indicates, the perceptron was intended as a model of perceptual activity. The aim of the perceptron was to associate input patterns (i.e., stimuli) with responses. This is equivalent to *recognizing* or *categorizing* the input patterns. Because of this, the perceptron is often seen as a *pattern recognition* device.

The main idea behind the design of the perceptron was that an object is first registered by the cells of the *retina* (i.e., the eye), and then *recognized* by cells located in the brain. The retinal cells are also called *input* cells. Typically these cells are binary cells: They can be either inactive (state 0) or active (state 1). The brain cells are called *associative* cells because their task is to associate patterns "seen" by the retina with the category to which they belong. They are also called *output* cells.

4

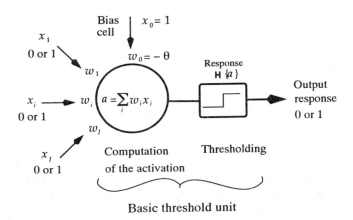

Basic threshold unit

Figure 2.1: A basic threshold unit computes its activation a as the weighted sum of its inputs. The response is equal to 0 if $a \leq 0$ and to 1 if $a > 0$.

2.2 The Building Block: The McCulloch and Pitts Neuron

Perceptrons are made of input cells connected to output cells. The output cells are similar to the *basic threshold units* described by McCulloch and Pitts (1943). Threshold units are very simple models of neurons, which can be interpreted as simple logical machines. They can be in one of two states: inactive or active (i.e., 0 or 1). The state of a threshold unit is determined by its degree of activation, which is, in turn, determined by integrating the information coming from several sources feeding to the device. Specifically (see Fig. 2.1), a threshold unit is linked to some input cells which can take only the values 0 and 1. A value 0 represents an inactive input cell, 1 an active cell. The input cells are connected to the neurons, and these connections are (loosely) identified as *synapses* (which connect real neurons). To each synapse is attached a *synaptic weight* (often simply called a weight). Each weight multiplies (i.e., magnifies or attenuates) the activity level of the connected input cell. A positive weight can be seen as excitatory and a negative weight as inhibitory. The basic threshold unit computes its activation as the sum of its (positive) excitation and of its (negative) inhibition coming from the active input cells (i.e., whose value is 1). If the activation is larger than some specified threshold, then the unit fires. This corresponds to transmitting an output value of 1. If the activation is smaller than the threshold, then the output value of the cell is 0.

More formally, the response of the threshold unit depends upon its level of activation, which is computed as the sum of the weights coming from active input cells. The response is then obtained by thresholding the activation (i.e., the cell will be in the active state only if its activation level is larger than a given threshold). Specifically, the activation of a threshold unit is computed as

$$a = \sum_i^I w_i x_i = w_1 x_1 + w_2 x_2 + \cdots + w_i x_i + \cdots + w_I x_I , \quad (2.1)$$

with $\sum_i^I$ the "summation" sign (read "sum from i to I"), a the activation of the unit, x_i the state of the ith input cell (0 or 1), I the number of input cells, and w_i the value of the weight connecting the ith input cell to the threshold unit.

The threshold unit will either be in the inactive state (i.e., give the response 0) if its level of activation is less than its threshold noted ϑ (the Greek letter "theta") or be in the active state (i.e., give the response 1) if its level of activation is greater than ϑ. Often, ϑ is simply set to 0. Formally, the response of the threshold unit is given by the so-called *Heaviside*, or *step* function, as

$$\text{response} = H\{a\} = \begin{cases} 0 & \text{for } a \leq \vartheta \\ 1 & \text{for } a > \vartheta \end{cases} . \quad (2.2)$$

The threshold can be seen as a weight. In this case, thresholding is implemented by keeping one input cell always active (the 0th input cell, sometimes called a *bias* cell) so that the weight w_0 is equal to $-\vartheta$. This is equivalent[1] to rewriting Eq. 2.2 as

$$\text{response} = \begin{cases} 0 & \text{for } a + w_0 \leq 0 \\ 1 & \text{for } a + w_0 > 0 \end{cases} \quad (2.3)$$

with w_0 being equal to $-\vartheta$. Equivalently, $w_0 = \vartheta$ if cell 0 is always set (i.e., "clamped") to the value -1. The term *response bias* is often used as a synonym for threshold.

2.2.1 Implementing Logical Functions

McCulloch and Pitts neurons have been used essentially to implement *logical functions*. A logical function is a function which associates a binary response (i.e., 0 or 1) to any pair of binary numbers.

---

[1]That is, the threshold is a quantity *subtracted* from the activation *before* the activation is transformed into a response.

TABLE 2.1

The logical function OR.

Binary Input Pattern		Binary Response
First Binary Number	Second Binary Number	
0	0	0
1	0	1
0	1	1
1	1	1

There are, in all, four different pairings of binary numbers, namely [0 0], [0 1], [1 0], and [1 1]. Therefore, a specific logical function is defined by a specific configuration of responses to these pairs of binary numbers. For example, the logical function OR given in Table 2.1 associates the response 0 to pattern [0 0] and the response 1 to patterns [1 0], [0 1], and [1 1]. There are in all $2^4 = 16$ possible logical functions (2 possible responses for the first pattern × 2 for the second pattern × 2 for the third pattern × 2 for the fourth pattern). Finding names for each function is a favorite pastime of logicians and neural modelers as well. The 16 logical functions are listed in Table 2.2.

A network with two input cells, one threshold unit, and weight values of $w_1 = 1$ and $w_2 = 1$ (any set of weights both being greater than 0 will work) can implement most logical functions. For example, as detailed in Table 2.3 on the next page, when presented with the input pattern $[x_1 \ x_2] = [0 \ 0]$ (i.e., both input cells are inactive), the threshold unit responds with the value 0. When presented with the input patterns $[x_1 \ x_2] = [0 \ 1]$, $[x_1 \ x_2] = [1 \ 0]$, or $[x_1 \ x_2] = [1 \ 1]$ (i.e., either one or both input cells are active), the output cell responds with the value 1. This configuration of responses corresponds to the OR function.

2.2.2 Learning From Examples

In the OR example, the weights were given. They could also have been determined fairly easily by trial and error. However, for complex patterns such an approach is cumbersome. As we show in the next sections, perceptrons can use a systematic procedure to find (or *learn* in the neural network jargon) the value of the weights appropriate for implementing a specific association.

TABLE 2.2

The 16 logical functions and some possible names (other names could be used, e.g., the "IF THEN" function is also called the "IMPLIES" function). The symbol $\sim$ denotes the negation (e.g., $\sim x_1$ is read "not x_1").

Value of Input Cell x_1	0	1	0	1	
Value of Input Cell x_2	0	0	1	1	
	Target Value for the Output Cell				Name of the Logical Function
	0	0	0	0	CONTRADICTION
	1	0	0	0	$\sim x_1$ AND $\sim x_2$
	0	1	0	0	x_1 AND ONLY x_1
	0	0	1	0	x_2 AND ONLY x_2
	0	0	0	1	x_1 AND x_2
	1	1	0	0	$\sim x_2$
	1	0	1	0	$\sim x_1$
	1	0	0	1	x_1 IF AND ONLY IF x_2
	0	1	1	0	x_1 XOR x_2
	0	1	0	1	x_1
	0	0	1	1	x_2
	1	1	1	0	$\sim x_1$ OR $\sim x_2$
	1	1	0	1	IF x_2 THEN x_1
	1	0	1	1	IF x_1 THEN x_2
	0	1	1	1	x_2 OR x_1
	1	1	1	1	TAUTOLOGY

TABLE 2.3

A threshold unit with $w_1 = 1$ and $w_2 = 1$ implements OR.

Input Values		Computation of the Activation of the Output Cell With $w_1 = 1$ and $w_2 = 1$	Response of the Output Cell
x_1	x_2	$a = w_1 x_1 + w_2 x_2$	
0	0	$(1 \times 0) + (1 \times 0) = 0$	0
1	0	$(1 \times 1) + (1 \times 0) = 1$	1
0	1	$(1 \times 0) + (1 \times 1) = 1$	1
1	1	$(1 \times 1) + (1 \times 1) = 2$	1

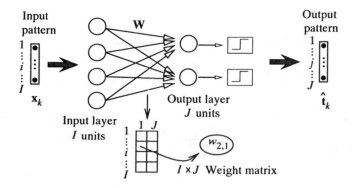

Figure 2.2: A perceptron with I input and J output units.

2.3 Architecture of a Perceptron

Formally, a perceptron is a network composed of I input units connected to J output basic units (see Fig. 2.2). Each output unit receives inputs from all the input units, sums them, and transforms the sum into a response using the Heaviside function. The set of connections between input and output units is given in an $I \times J$ matrix $\mathbf{W}$:

$$\mathbf{W} = \begin{bmatrix} w_{1,1} & w_{1,2} & \cdots & w_{1,J} \\ w_{2,1} & w_{2,2} & \cdots & w_{2,J} \\ \vdots & \vdots & \ddots & \vdots \\ w_{I,1} & w_{I,2} & \cdots & w_{I,J} \end{bmatrix}. \tag{2.4}$$

In this matrix, a given element $w_{i,j}$ represents the strength of the connection between the ith input unit and the jth output unit.

There are K input patterns. Each input pattern is represented by an I-dimensional vector denoted $\mathbf{x}_k$. Each of the K corresponding output patterns (i.e., *targets*) is represented by a J-dimensional vector denoted $\mathbf{t}_k$. Learning of the mapping between input-output pairs is done by modifying the strength of the connections between input and output units. The response for stimulus $\mathbf{x}_k$ is a $J \times 1$ vector, denoted $\widehat{\mathbf{t}}_k$ (the "hat" indicates that it estimates the target $\mathbf{t}_k$), equal to

$$\widehat{\mathbf{t}}_k = \mathsf{H}\{\mathbf{W}^T \mathbf{x}_k\}, \tag{2.5}$$

where ^{T} is the transpose operation (it reverses the rows and the columns of a matrix); the Heaviside function is applied elementwise.

Several learning rules can be used to adjust the connection weights. The best known rule goes by a number of names: the *Widrow-Hoff* rule (Duda & Hart, 1973; we use this term here), the *Delta* rule, or simply the *perceptron learning* rule.

2.4 The Widrow-Hoff Learning Rule

2.4.1 General Principle

Because the synaptic weights control the response of the output cell, the principal problem for the perceptron is to "discover" what weight values can accomplish a specific task. Essentially, a perceptron output cell "learns" by adapting (i.e., changing) its weights when the response it gives does not correspond to the response that was expected: The perceptron learns only when it makes mistakes.

In order to learn, the perceptron needs to know when it has made a mistake and what response it should have given. This is called *supervised learning*. The learning rule is local in the sense that each output cell learns without needing to know the response of the other output cells. Only the information coming from the retinal cells is important. The application of the rule itself is rather simple in the case of the perceptron. Each time a cell makes a mistake, it changes its synaptic weights in order to make the error less likely to occur if the same stimulus is presented again. In summary, the main idea behind Widrow-Hoff learning can be expressed in a way that sounds quite like parental advice:

> With Widrow-Hoff learning, when you make a mistake, pay less attention to the input cells that told you to make this mistake, and pay more attention to the input cells that told you not to make this mistake.

Two types of errors might occur during learning: Either the output cell is inactive when it should have been active, or the output cell is active when it should have been inactive.

Let us consider the *first case*. The output cell is inactive but should have been active. This means that the activation value of the output cell is negative (supposing the threshold is zero). This negative activation is obtained because the sum of the positive synaptic weights associated to active input cells is *less* important than the sum of the negative synaptic weights (recall that because the inactive cells have an input value of 0 they do not contribute to the activation). In other words, the output cell is paying too much attention to the input cells telling it to be inactive and not enough attention to the input cells telling it to be active. An obvious correction to this is to give less importance to the active input cells with a negative synaptic weight and more importance to the active input cells with a positive synaptic weight. This can be achieved by *adding* a small positive quantity to all the synaptic weights of the active input cells. By so doing, the activation will be more positive the next time the same stimulus is presented.

The *second type* of error occurs when the output cell is active but should have been inactive. It is active because its activation level is positive. This positive activation is obtained because the sum of the positive synaptic weights associated to active input cells is *more* important than the sum of the negative synaptic weights associated to active input cells. In other words, the output cell is paying too much attention to the input cells telling it to be active and not enough attention to the input cells telling it to be inactive. An obvious correction to this is to give less importance to the active input cells with a positive synaptic weight and more importance to the active input cells with a negative synaptic weight. This can be achieved by *subtracting* a small positive quantity from (or equivalently, by *adding* a small *negative* quantity to) all the synaptic weights of the active input cells. This will make the positive weights less important and the negative weights more important. By so doing, the activation will be less positive the next time the same stimulus is presented.

2.4.2 A Little Bit of Math

The Widrow-Hoff learning rule proceeds by iterations: The set of patterns to be learned is presented (in a random order in general) to the perceptron and each pattern is learned in turn. Learning one pattern is called a learning *iteration*; learning the full set of patterns is called a learning *epoch*, or a *sweep* by some authors. If after the first epoch the perceptron still makes mistakes, a new epoch starts (with another arbitrary order), and the perceptron continues learning. The procedure is repeated until the perceptron gives all correct responses.

Learning is achieved by adding, to the weights of the active input cells, a small quantity that is denoted $\Delta_{w_{i,j}}$ (read "Delta of $w_{i,j}$"). This quantity takes into account the state of the input cell as well as the error made by the output cell. The Widrow-Hoff learning rule specifies the correction to apply, at iteration n, to the weight connecting the ith input cell to the jth output cell as

$$w_{i,j}^{(n+1)} = w_{i,j}^{(n)} + \eta(t_j - \widehat{t}_j)x_i = w_{i,j}^{(n)} + \Delta_{w_{i,j}} , \qquad (2.6)$$

with n the iteration number; $\Delta_{w_{i,j}}$ the change to be made in the value $w_{i,j}$; x_i the activation value (0 or 1) of the ith retinal cell; $\widehat{t}_j$ (read "t hat") the response (0 or 1) of the jth output cell; t_j the *target* value, or desired response (0 or 1) of the jth output cell; $(t_j - \hat{t}_j)$ the *error* made by the jth output cell; $w_{i,j}^{(n)}$ the intensity of the connection between the ith input cell and the jth output cell at iteration n (the initial values $w_{i,j}^{(0)}$ are generally chosen randomly); and η (the Greek letter "eta") a positive constant, generally between 0 and 1. It corresponds to the small positive constant to be added to or subtracted from the synaptic weights. Selecting a value for η is often delicate because it influences the speed of learning. A possible value could be .75. In some cases, η could vary as a function of n (the iteration index). In that case, learning would start with a high value of η (say .90) and then η would decrease with each iteration (or each epoch). How to choose the value of η is treated in greater detail in Chapter 3.

Let us have a closer look at Eq. 2.6 and see that it amounts to doing what we described previously. When the output cell gives the correct response, the values of the target (t_j) and the output $(\hat{t}_j)$ are the same, which makes the term $\eta(t_j - \hat{t}_j)x_i$ equal to 0. Therefore, there is no correction when the perceptron gives the correct response. When the input cells are inactive, the term x_i is equal to zero, and so the term $\eta(t_j - \hat{t}_j)x_i$ is also equal to zero. Therefore, the synaptic weights of inactive cells are left unchanged. If the output cell is inactive when it should be active, the term $(t_j - \hat{t}_j)$ is equal to $(1-0) = 1$ and the change made to the synaptic weights of the active input cells amounts to adding the small positive constant η to them. If the output cell is active when it should be inactive, the term $(t_j - \hat{t}_j)$ is equal to $(0 - 1) = -1$ and the change made to the synaptic weights of the active input cells amounts to subtracting the small positive constant η from them. In addition to being concise and elegant, Eq. 2.6 is very general and is easily extended to more complex neural networks.

2.4.3 Matrix Notation for the Widrow-Hoff Learning Rule

Eq. 2.6 on the facing page describing Widrow-Hoff learning can be rewritten using matrix notation to specify the correction to apply to the complete set of weights after one iteration (i.e., after presentation of pattern k):

$$\mathbf{W}_{[n+1]}^T = \mathbf{W}_{[n]}^T + \eta(\mathbf{t}_k - \hat{\mathbf{t}}_k)\mathbf{x}_k^T = \mathbf{W}_{[n]}^T + \eta(\mathbf{t}_k - \mathrm{H}\{\mathbf{W}_{[n]}^T\mathbf{x}_k\})\mathbf{x}_k^T$$
$$= \mathbf{W}_{[n]}^T + \Delta\mathbf{w}_{[n]}, \tag{2.7}$$

where n represents the iteration number; η a small positive constant; $\mathbf{x}_k$ the $I \times 1$ kth input vector; $\mathbf{t}_k$ the $J \times 1$ kth target vector; $\hat{\mathbf{t}}_k$ the

$J \times 1$ kth response vector; $\boldsymbol{\Delta}_{\mathbf{W}_{[n]}}$ the matrix of corrections for $\mathbf{W}$ at the nth iteration; and k a random integer $(1 \leq k \leq K)$.

2.4.4 A Numerical Example: Learning OR

Suppose that we want to teach a perceptron the logical function OR, whose truth table is

$$
\begin{array}{ccc}
0 \quad 0 & \longmapsto & 0 \\
1 \quad 0 & \longmapsto & 1 \\
0 \quad 1 & \longmapsto & 1 \\
1 \quad 1 & \longmapsto & 1 .
\end{array} \tag{2.8}
$$

This perceptron is composed of three input cells: two cells for the values of the argument of the logical function, plus one cell (i.e., x_0) to implement thresholding, and one output cell (see Fig. 2.1 on page 4). This is equivalent to implementing the following ternary truth table:

$$
\begin{array}{lll}
\mathbf{x}_1^T = [1 \quad 0 \quad 0] & \longmapsto & 0 \\
\mathbf{x}_2^T = [1 \quad 1 \quad 0] & \longmapsto & 1 \\
\mathbf{x}_3^T = [1 \quad 0 \quad 1] & \longmapsto & 1 \\
\mathbf{x}_4^T = [1 \quad 1 \quad 1] & \longmapsto & 1 .
\end{array}
$$

Assuming that the synaptic weights (i.e., the w_i's) are initialized to zero values, they can be represented by a 3×1 matrix[2] $\mathbf{w}_{[0]}$:

$$
\mathbf{w}_{[0]} = \begin{bmatrix} w_0 = -\vartheta \\ w_1 \\ w_2 \end{bmatrix} = \begin{bmatrix} 0 \\ 0 \\ 0 \end{bmatrix} .
$$

Suppose, now, that the first randomly chosen association is the fourth one (i.e., the perceptron should produce the value 1 when its retinal cells are presented with the stimulus $[1\ 1\ 1]$). The activation of the output cell is given by

$$
a = \mathbf{w}_{[0]}^T \mathbf{x}_4 = \sum_i w_i x_i = (0 \times 1) + (0 \times 1) + (0 \times 1) = 0 .
$$

---

[2]Because there is only one output cell, the weight matrix is, in fact, a *vector* (i.e., a matrix with only one column) which we will denote by $\mathbf{w}$. The notation is also somewhat simpler; for example, $w_{i,j}$ becomes w_i.

The (incorrect) response of the perceptron is (*cf.* Eq. 2.2 on page 5): $\hat{t} = H\{a\} = H\{0\} = 0$.

The error is the difference between the target value ($t = 1$) and the response of the output cell ($\hat{t} = 0$). Supposing that $\eta = .1$, the correction for the synapses from the retinal cells to the output cell is

$$\Delta_{w_0} = \eta(t - \hat{t})x_0 = .1 \times (1 - 0) \times 1 = .1$$
$$\Delta_{w_1} = \eta(t - \hat{t})x_1 = .1 \times (1 - 0) \times 1 = .1$$
$$\Delta_{w_2} = \eta(t - \hat{t})x_2 = .1 \times (1 - 0) \times 1 = .1 .$$

After the correction has been applied, $\mathbf{w}_{[0]}$ becomes $\mathbf{w}_{[1]}$:

$$\mathbf{w}_{[1]} = \mathbf{w}_{[0]} + \Delta_{\mathbf{w}_{[0]}} = \begin{bmatrix} w_0 = 0 \\ w_1 = 0 \\ w_2 = 0 \end{bmatrix} + \begin{bmatrix} \Delta_{w_0} = .1 \\ \Delta_{w_1} = .1 \\ \Delta_{w_2} = .1 \end{bmatrix} = \begin{bmatrix} w_0 = .1 \\ w_1 = .1 \\ w_2 = .1 \end{bmatrix} .$$

Suppose, now, that the first stimulus (i.e., [1 0 0]) is presented to the perceptron. The activation of the output cell is given by

$$a = \mathbf{w}_{[1]}^T \mathbf{x}_1 = \sum_i w_i x_i = (.1 \times 1) + (.1 \times 0) + (.1 \times 0) = .1 ,$$

and the response of the output cell is: $\hat{t} = H\{a\} = H\{.1\} = 1$. The correction to apply to the synaptic weights is

$$\Delta_{w_0} = \eta(t - \hat{t})x_0 = .1 \times (0 - 1) \times 1 = -.1$$
$$\Delta_{w_1} = \eta(t - \hat{t})x_1 = .1 \times (0 - 1) \times 0 = 0$$
$$\Delta_{w_2} = \eta(t - \hat{t})x_2 = .1 \times (0 - 1) \times 0 = 0 .$$

After the error correction rule has been applied, $\mathbf{w}_{[1]}$ becomes $\mathbf{w}_{[2]}$:

$$\mathbf{w}_{[2]} = \mathbf{w}_{[1]} + \Delta_{\mathbf{w}_{[1]}} = \begin{bmatrix} w_0 = .1 \\ w_1 = .1 \\ w_2 = .1 \end{bmatrix} + \begin{bmatrix} \Delta_{w_0} = -.1 \\ \Delta_{w_1} = 0 \\ \Delta_{w_2} = 0 \end{bmatrix} = \begin{bmatrix} w_0 = 0 \\ w_1 = .1 \\ w_2 = .1 \end{bmatrix} .$$

With this set of weights, the perceptron implements OR.

2.5 Learning With $+1/-1$ Cells

So far the input cells have taken only two values, 1 and 0, to model the active vs. inactive (i.e., *on* and *off*) state of a neuron. An alternative approach would be to have three possible states for the input cells: +1, 0, and −1. If we think of an input cell as a feature detector, this is equivalent to having the possibility of representing cases such as *yes* (feature present), *no* (feature absent), and *don't know* (no information available). These cases will be coded respectively as +1, −1, and 0. An alternative interpretation, more in tune with a neural point of view, is to consider that the value +1 models *excitation*, the value −1 models *inhibition*, and the value 0 models an inactive state. Assigning values of +1 and −1 is also useful when dealing with features that are *essentially* binary.

As an example of ternary input cells, suppose that you want to represent whether a person is smiling or frowning. With a 1/0 coding schema (representing smiling as 1 and frowning as 0), only the smile will lead to a correction of the connection weights when an output cell is in error. In other words, the 1/0 coding schema implies an *asymmetry* between the active state and the inactive state. One possible way of representing binary features such as *smiling/frowning* is to use *two* cells per feature: the first one coding the smile, and the second one coding the frown. Using such a coding schema, a smile will be represented with the first cell active and the second cell inactive, whereas a frown will be represented with the first cell inactive and the second cell active. When the person is neither smiling nor frowning (or if the information about the mouth is unavailable), both cells will be inactive. An alternative approach is simply to use the +1, 0, −1 coding schema with one cell. In this case, a smile will be represented by the cell taking a value of +1, and a frown will be represented by the cell taking a value of −1. When the person is neither smiling nor frowning, the cell will take the value of zero. This will lead to equivalent performance but with half the number of cells. Interestingly, Eqs. 2.6 (page 10) and 2.7 (page 11) describing Widrow-Hoff learning work with ternary input cells as well as with binary input cells. Actually, these equations will also work for input cells taking real values.

2.5.1 A Numerical Example: Girls and Boys

Suppose you want to train a ternary perceptron to categorize the schematic faces presented in Fig. 2.3 as girls and boys. Each face is made of five features (hair, eyes, nose, mouth, and ears), each taking either the value +1 or −1 (see Fig. 2.4), and can be represented by a 5-dimensional vector $\mathbf{x}_k$. For example, the first face is represented by

$$\mathbf{x}_1^T = [x_{1,1} \quad x_{2,1} \quad x_{3,1} \quad x_{4,1} \quad x_{5,1}] = [+1 \quad +1 \quad +1 \quad -1 \quad -1].$$

The girls

[+1,+1,+1,-1,-1]   [+1,-1,+1,+1,+1]   [-1,+1,-1,+1,+1]

The boys

[-1,-1,+1,-1,-1]   [-1,+1,-1,+1,-1]   [+1,-1,+1,-1,-1]

Figure 2.3: Three boys and three girls. The vector below each face corresponds to the feature values for this face. The elements of the vectors correspond to the following features [Hair, Eyes, Nose, Mouth, Ear].

FEATURE	LEVEL +1	-1	CELL
Hair		(((	1
Eyes	• •	ᵕ ᵕ	2
Nose	ı	L	3
Mouth	‿	—	4
Ears	ʃ ʔ	6 ɘ	5

Figure 2.4: The five features used to describe the faces in Fig. 2.3.

The first element of $\mathbf{x}_1$ (i.e., $x_{1,1}$), equal to $+1$, indicates that the first feature of the first face (the hair) takes on the value $+1$. Similarly, the second element of $\mathbf{x}_1$ (i.e., $x_{2,1}$) indicates that the second feature of the first face (the eyes) takes the value $+1$, and so on.

Each cell of the perceptron corresponds to one of the five features describing the face and will take on the value of this feature (or a value of 0 if the value of the feature is unavailable). Hence, a perceptron with five (ternary) input cells and one output cell can learn to categorize girls and boys. The girls will correspond to a target value of 1 and the boys to 0. As illustrated in Table 2.4, with a value of the learning constant η equal to 1, the perceptron needs three iterations to learn to correctly categorize girls and boys (when all the features are present). The final weight vector is equal to $\mathbf{w} =$

TABLE 2.4

The first three iterations of a perceptron learning to categorize the faces from Fig. 2.3. The target value is 1 for the girls and 0 for the boys. The learning constant η is equal to 1. After the third iteration the perceptron correctly classifies boys and girls (see Table 2.5). The symbol **w** is the weight vector, **x** is the input pattern, a is the activation value of the output cell, $\hat{t}$ is the output value of the output cell, t is the target value, and $e = (t - \hat{t})$ is the error made by the output cell.

Iteration	$\mathbf{w}^T$	$\mathbf{x}$	a	$\hat{t}$	t	e	new $\mathbf{w}^T$
1	[0 0 0 0 0]	[1 1 1 −1 −1]^T	0	0	1	1	[1 1 1 −1 −1]
2	[1 1 1 −1 −1]	[1 1 −1 1 1]^T	−1	0	1	1	[2 0 2 0 0]
3	[2 0 2 0 0]	[−1 1 −1 1 1]^T	−4	0	1	1	[1 1 1 1 1]

TABLE 2.5

Response of the perceptron when $\mathbf{w} = \begin{bmatrix} 1 & 1 & 1 & 1 & 1 \end{bmatrix}^T$.

x (input)					a	$\widehat{t}$	t
The Girls						$(t = 1)$	
$[\ 1$	1	1	-1	$-1]^T$	1	1	1
$[\ 1$	-1	1	1	$1]^T$	3	1	1
$[-1$	1	-1	1	$1]^T$	1	1	1
The Boys						$(t = 0)$	
$[-1$	-1	1	-1	$-1]^T$	-3	0	0
$[-1$	1	-1	1	$-1]^T$	-1	0	0
$[\ 1$	-1	1	-1	$-1]^T$	-1	0	0

$\begin{bmatrix} 1 & 1 & 1 & 1 & 1 \end{bmatrix}^T$. Actually, with this weight vector the categorization decision of the perceptron is equivalent to counting the number of positive feature values for the faces. If there are more positive features than negative ones, then the face is categorized as a girl; otherwise it is categorized as a boy. If the value of a feature is missing, the perceptron is still able to make a decision. Most of the time the decision reached will correspond to a correct classification because girls have mostly positive features, whereas boys have mostly negative features.

2.6 Performance Evaluation

So far we have shown that the perceptron is able to learn logical functions, such as the OR function, or to solve some simple categorization tasks like separating boys from girls. But is it able to learn all the logical functions or to solve more complex categorization problems?

2.6.1 The XOR Problem

Of the 16 logical functions (*cf.* Section 2.2.1 on page 5), 14 can be learned by a perceptron. The two logical functions that a perceptron cannot learn are XOR and its complement IF AND ONLY IF (see Table 2.2). To show this, consider the XOR function, and suppose that we have a perceptron with two input cells and one output cell. The synaptic weights are noted w_1 and w_2. The association of the input pattern [1 0] to the response 1 implies that $w_1 > \vartheta$. Similarly, the association of the input pattern [0 1] to the response 1 implies that $w_2 > \vartheta$. Adding together these two inequalities gives $w_1 + w_2 > \vartheta$. Now, if the threshold unit gives the response 0 to the input pattern [1 1], this implies that $w_1 + w_2 \leq \vartheta$. Clearly, the sum $w_1 + w_2$ cannot be at the same time larger than and smaller than (or equal to) ϑ. Therefore no set of weights can solve the XOR problem.

2.6.2 Perceptron and Linear Separability

If a function can be learned by a perceptron, then there is at least one weight vector **w** such that the scalar[3] product $\mathbf{w}^T\mathbf{x}$ is positive for all the members of one category (i.e., the "1" category) and negative for all the members of the other category. This amounts to separating the set of all the possible input vectors (called the *input space*) into two subspaces. The surface separating the two subspaces is called a *decision boundary* or a *decision surface*. Its position is specified by the equation $\mathbf{w}^T\mathbf{x} = 0$.

This equation determines a linear surface with dimension one less than the dimension of the input space. For example, if the input space is 2-dimensional (i.e., a plane), the decision boundary is a straight line; if the input space is 3-dimensional, the decision boundary is a plane. In general, if the input space is n-dimensional, the decision boundary is an $(n - 1)$-dimensional *hyperplane*. As a consequence, a classification which can be learned by a one-cell perceptron is called *linearly separable* (because there is a *linear* surface separating the categories). We have seen that among the 16 logical functions, 14 are linearly separable, and 2 are *nonlinearly separable* (the XOR and IF AND ONLY IF functions). As an illustration, Fig. 2.5 on the facing page shows that the 0 and 1 responses of the XOR and the IF AND ONLY IF functions cannot be separated by a line but that the 0 and 1 responses of the OR function can. When the categories are linearly separable, the convergence of the perceptron is guaranteed (see Hertz, Krogh, & Palmer, 1991).

The 2-dimensional case (illustrated by the logical functions) is somewhat misleading because it suggests that there are more linearly separable than nonlinearly separable functions. This is, in general, not true: For any number of input units larger than three, the

---

[3]The *scalar* product (also called *dot* or *inner* product) of two vectors associates a scalar (i.e., a number) to two vectors having the same number of elements. The scalar product of vectors **w** and **x** is noted $\mathbf{w}^T\mathbf{x}$ and is computed as $\mathbf{w}^T\mathbf{x} = \sum_{i}^{I} w_i x_i$ (where I is the number of elements of **w** and **x**).

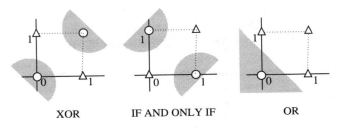

Figure 2.5: XOR and IF AND ONLY IF are not linearly separable, but OR is.

number of nonlinearly separable functions is larger than the number of linearly separable functions. In fact, the ratio of the number of linearly separable functions to the number of nonlinearly separable functions tends toward 0 as the number of input units grows (e.g., Hassoun, 1995).

2.6.3 Learning Nonlinear Classifications with a Perceptron

The decision boundaries of the standard perceptron are linear. It is, nevertheless, possible to create nonlinear boundaries with a perceptron. Specifically, a perceptron can learn polynomial decision boundaries if some input cells are used to code the *product* of the features describing the patterns. For example, the XOR function can be learned by a three-input cell perceptron, with the third cell giving the product of the first two cells. This is equivalent to learning the association

$$
\begin{array}{ccccc}
0 & 0 & 0 & \longmapsto & 0 \\
1 & 0 & 0 & \longmapsto & 1 \\
0 & 1 & 0 & \longmapsto & 1 \\
1 & 1 & 1 & \longmapsto & 0 \,.
\end{array}
\tag{2.9}
$$

2.7 The Perceptron and Discriminant Analysis

The perceptron is closely related to the statistical technique of *discriminant analysis*. In the particular case of two groups, discriminant analysis uses a *linear discriminant function* to classify input patterns into two classes. The linear discriminant function is defined as an $I \times 1$ weight vector[4] $\mathbf{v}$ such that for each input pattern $\mathbf{x}_k$, a target

---

[4]If the first element of each input pattern is set to a constant value (e.g., -1), it plays a role equivalent to a threshold for the perceptron. We assume, in this discussion, that this procedure is used.

value $\widehat{y}_k$ is obtained as $\widehat{y}_k = \mathbf{v}^T \mathbf{x}_k$. If $\widehat{y}_k > 0$, the pattern $\mathbf{x}_k$ is classified as a member of the first class; otherwise $\mathbf{x}_k$ is classified as a member of the second class. The similarity of this equation to Eq. 2.5 on page 8 suggests that linear discriminant analysis and the perceptron are related techniques. This is indeed the case, but they are, however, not identical because their weight vectors are set to meet different criteria. Each criterion can be expressed as finding a minimum value for an error function. It can be shown (Duda & Hart, 1973, p. 141) that the perceptron procedure finds a vector $\mathbf{w}$ corresponding to the minimum of the error function:

$$\mathcal{J} = \sum_k \left| (t_k - \widehat{t}_k) \mathbf{w}^T \mathbf{x}_k \right| . \qquad (2.10)$$

Discriminant analysis, by contrast, finds a vector $\mathbf{v}$ corresponding to the minimum of the error function

$$\mathcal{J} = \frac{1}{2} \sum_k (y_k - \widehat{y}_k)^2 = \frac{1}{2} \sum_k (y_k - \mathbf{v}^T \mathbf{x}_k)^2 \qquad (2.11)$$

where the values y_k are set to $+1$ for the first class and to -1 for the second class (supposing that the classes have the same number of elements; see also Section 4.7 on page 60).

2.8 Learning and Testing Sets: The Validation Problem

The distinction between sample and population, so important for inferential statistics, is also relevant for neural networks. Contrary to discriminant analysis, which can be shown, under the proper assumptions, to be the best linear unbiased estimator for the parameters of the best classifier of the population, the perceptron is optimal *only* for the sample used for training. This is a direct consequence of the perceptron learning rule: The perceptron learns only when a misclassification occurs.

In order to evaluate the performance of the perceptron on a potential population, the standard parametric inferential techniques do not work (i.e., the perceptron is a *nonparametric classifier*). To estimate the generalization performance of the perceptron, a *testing* set different from the *learning* set is often used. Other procedures such as *bootstrap* or *jackknife* are also often used. These techniques are used when only a small set of patterns is available. The main idea here is to learn a classification on a subset of the patterns and to test the generalization on the remaining patterns (the jackknife uses all patterns but one to learn and tests on the remaining one, as its nickname of "leave one out" indicates). The procedure is repeated for several learning subsets, and the average performance gives a nonparametric estimation of the generalization potential.

3. LINEAR AUTOASSOCIATIVE MEMORIES

3.1 Overview

Autoassociative memories are single-layer networks made of fully interconnected linear units that operate in parallel. A *linear* unit is a very simple unit whose output is proportional to its level of activation (it is called *linear* because the output is a linear function of the activation). The goal of an autoassociative memory is to store a set of stimuli (i.e., each stimulus is associated with itself and added to the memory) and to retrieve the stored stimuli when cued with partial or degraded versions of these stimuli.

Because the representation of individual stimuli is not localized in the memory but distributed throughout the entire network, an autoassociative memory is "content addressable." In contrast to a classical computer, which uses the exact location or memory address to retrieve stored information, an autoassociative memory is able to retrieve a whole pattern of information given only part of this information. For example, Kohonen (1977) showed that an autoassociative memory could act as a content addressable memory for face images. In his demonstration, an autoassociative memory was first created by autoassociating a set of 100 face images represented as arrays of pixel intensities. The memory was then tested by presenting incomplete face images as input. Results showed that the images reconstructed by the system were convincingly similar to the original images (see Fig. 3.1 for an illustration).

Because of this property, autoassociative memories are widely used in many pattern recognition applications and for modeling human perceptual learning and memory. From a modeling point of view their interest stems from the fact that they are easily analyzable in terms of traditional mathematical concepts and statistical techniques (i.e., least squares estimation, singular value decomposition, and principal component analysis). Autoassociative memories can give rise to a number of testable behavioral predictions. In addition,

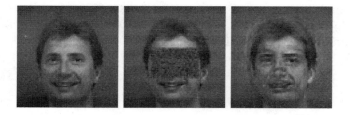

Figure 3.1: Illustration of a content addressable memory for faces. Images of faces were stored using an autoassociative memory. The left panel shows a stimulus stored into the memory. The center panel shows the stimulus given as a key (i.e., a cue) to probe the memory. The right panel shows the response of the memory. The memory is able to reconstruct, reasonably well, a face from an incomplete input.

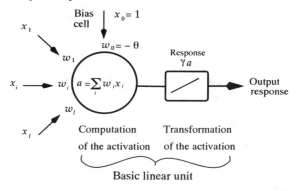

Figure 3.2: A basic linear unit computes its activation a as the weighted sum of its inputs. The output response is proportional to the activation.

they are reminiscent of our ability to produce a correct response, even when prompted by incomplete or somewhat erroneous cues (because we use context to "fill in" the gaps). For example, you will probably have no problem answering the following question: How many animals of each species did Moses take on the ark to protect them from the flood? You might not even have noticed that the question was incorrect (*Noah*, not *Moses*, took the animals on the ark).

3.2 The Building Block: The Basic Linear Unit

Linear autoassociative memories are built from *linear units* fully interconnected. A linear unit is quite similar to the basic threshold unit presented in Chapter 2. Its activation is computed in the same manner. Actually, the only difference is the transfer function used to transform the activation into a response.

The linear unit computes its activation level by adding all the weighted external activation values. Then, it transforms this activation into a *response* or an *output*. This transformation, called a *linear transfer function*, makes the output proportional to the activation. In brief: A linear unit (see Fig. 3.2) computes its activation level as the weighted sum of its inputs. A linear transfer function transforms its activation into its output.

Formally, if a unit has I inputs[1] noted $x_1, \ldots, x_i, \ldots, x_I$, each of them connected with a weight denoted w_i, the activation of the cell will be computed as

$$a = \sum_i^I w_i x_i \qquad (3.1)$$

and the response of the cell will be equal to γa (with γ, read "gamma," being a constant). Using vector notation, if $\mathbf{x}$ is the input vector and $\mathbf{w}$ the weight vector, the activation of the cell is computed as

$$a = \sum_i^I w_i x_i = \mathbf{w}^T \mathbf{x}, \qquad (3.2)$$

where $\mathbf{w}^T \mathbf{x}$ is the scalar product of vectors $\mathbf{w}$ and $\mathbf{x}$. The output, or response of the cell, being proportional to its activation, is therefore computed as

$$\text{response} = \gamma a = \gamma \mathbf{w}^T \mathbf{x}. \qquad (3.3)$$

Learning occurs by changing the values of the synaptic weights.

3.3 Architecture of an Autoassociative Memory

An autoassociative memory is a network of I linear units or cells fully interconnected (i.e., each cell is connected to all other cells and also to itself) by modifiable connections or synapses (see Fig. 3.3).

---

[1] To add a threshold, we proceed as for the perceptron by adding a fictitious x_0 cell with a constant output of -1. The weight w_0 is the threshold (see page 5).

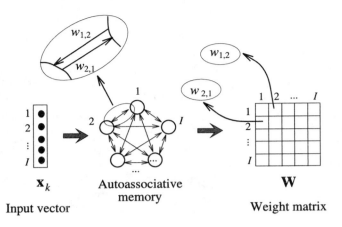

Figure 3.3: An autoassociative memory composed of I cells.

The set of connections is stored in a square matrix $\mathbf{W}$:

$$\mathbf{W} = \begin{bmatrix} w_{1,1} & w_{1,2} & \cdots & w_{1,I} \\ w_{2,1} & w_{2,2} & \cdots & w_{2,I} \\ \vdots & \vdots & \vdots & \vdots \\ w_{I,1} & w_{I,2} & \cdots & w_{I,I} \end{bmatrix} . \tag{3.4}$$

In this matrix a given element $w_{i,i'}$ represents the strength of the connection between cell i and cell i'. The connections between two cells i and i' are bidirectional and generally symmetrical (i.e., $w_{i,i'} = w_{i',i}$). Each of the K objects to be stored in the memory is represented by an I-dimensional vector denoted $\mathbf{x}_k$ in which a given element corresponds to a feature describing the pattern. Each element in these vectors is used as input to a cell of the autoassociative memory. The set of K input patterns is represented by an $I \times K$ matrix $\mathbf{X}$ whose kth column is $\mathbf{x}_k$ and whose generic element $x_{i,k}$ represents the value of the ith feature of the kth pattern.

Learning results from the modification of the value of the connections following the presentation of a set of patterns. These modifications can be implemented using two different learning rules. The first one, the *Hebbian learning rule*, requires minimal computation. It is generally described as "unsupervised," because no feedback concerning the correctness of a response is provided during the learning process.[2] The second one, the *Widrow-Hoff learning rule*, requires

---

[2]However, as mentioned in Chapter 4, Hebbian learning may sometimes be considered as supervised.

more computation and time. It is essentially the same technique that we have seen in Chapter 2.

3.4 The Hebbian Learning Rule

The Hebbian learning rule is based on work by Donald Hebb, who theorized that learning is a purely local phenomenon expressible in terms of synaptic change. Specifically, the synaptic change depends on both presynaptic and postsynaptic activities such that

> When an axon of cell A is near enough to excite a cell B and repeatedly or persistently takes part in firing it, some growth process or metabolic change takes place in one or both cells such that A's efficiency as one of the cells firing B, is increased. (Hebb, 1949; p. 62)

Hebb's learning rule states that the change in synaptic strength is a function of the temporal correlation between presynaptic and post-synaptic activities. Specifically, the synaptic strength between two neurons A and B increases whenever the two neurons are in the same state and decreases when they are in different states. In brief:

> With Hebbian learning, the connection between two neurons is proportional to the (temporal) correlation of their activation values during learning.

3.4.1 Hebb Rule and Associative Learning

The Hebbian learning rule sets the change of the connection weight between two cells to be proportional to the product of their activity at the time of learning. More formally, a set of K patterns is stored in a linear autoassociative memory by multiplying each pattern vector by its transpose and summing the resulting outer-product matrices. This learning rule is defined as

$$\mathbf{W} = \gamma \sum_{k=1}^{K} \mathbf{x}_k \mathbf{x}_k^T, \tag{3.5}$$

where γ is the proportionality constant. Often, for convenience, γ is set to 1. We will follow this tradition in this chapter.

Figure 3.4: Schematic faces for Hebbian learning. Each face is made of four features (hair, eyes, nose, and mouth), taking the value +1 or −1.

		LEVEL		
FEATURE	+1		-1	CELL
Hair			(((	1
Eyes	• •		ᴗ ᴗ	2
Nose	ı		L	3
Mouth	⌣		—	4

Figure 3.5: The features used to build the faces in Fig. 3.4.

3.4.2 A Numerical Example

Imagine that you want to store the set of schematic faces presented in Fig. 3.4 in an autoassociative memory using Hebbian learning. Each face is represented by a 4-dimensional binary vector, denoted $\mathbf{x}_k$, in which a given element corresponds to one of the features from Fig. 3.5. For example, the first face in Fig. 3.4 is represented by the vector $\mathbf{x}_1^T = [+1 \quad +1 \quad +1 \quad -1]$.

To store a face in the autoassociative memory, each element of the face vector $\mathbf{x}_k$ is used as input to a cell of the memory and each cell is connected to every other cell of the memory (including itself). The values of the connection strengths between the cells of the memory are stored in the 4×4 matrix $\mathbf{W}$. For convenience, we assume that the connection strengths are initialized with zero values:

$$\mathbf{W}_{[0]} = \begin{bmatrix} 0 & 0 & 0 & 0 \\ 0 & 0 & 0 & 0 \\ 0 & 0 & 0 & 0 \\ 0 & 0 & 0 & 0 \end{bmatrix}.$$

Step 1: The first face is stored in the memory by modifying the values of the connection weights according to Eq. 3.5:

$$\mathbf{W}_{[1]} = \mathbf{W}_{[0]} + \mathbf{x}_1\mathbf{x}_1^T$$

$$= \begin{bmatrix} 0 & 0 & 0 & 0 \\ 0 & 0 & 0 & 0 \\ 0 & 0 & 0 & 0 \\ 0 & 0 & 0 & 0 \end{bmatrix} + \begin{bmatrix} +1 \\ +1 \\ +1 \\ -1 \end{bmatrix} \times [\; +1 \quad +1 \quad +1 \quad -1\;]$$

$$= \begin{bmatrix} +1 & +1 & +1 & -1 \\ +1 & +1 & +1 & -1 \\ +1 & +1 & +1 & -1 \\ -1 & -1 & -1 & +1 \end{bmatrix}.$$

Examining the weight matrix obtained after storing the first face shows that each time two features take the same value ($+1$ or -1), the strength of the connection between the two cells of the memory corresponding to those features is equal to $+1$. In contrast, each time two features take different values ($+1$ and -1 or -1 and $+1$), the strength of the connection between the two cells of the memory corresponding to those features is equal to -1. In other words, the weight matrix is proportional to the covariance[3] among features.

Step 2: The second face, represented by $\mathbf{x}_2^T = [-1 \quad -1 \quad +1 \quad -1]$, is stored in the memory in addition to the first one:

$$\mathbf{W}_{[2]} = \mathbf{W}_{[1]} + \mathbf{x}_2\mathbf{x}_2^T$$

$$= \begin{bmatrix} +1 & +1 & +1 & -1 \\ +1 & +1 & +1 & -1 \\ +1 & +1 & +1 & -1 \\ -1 & -1 & -1 & +1 \end{bmatrix} + \begin{bmatrix} -1 \\ -1 \\ +1 \\ -1 \end{bmatrix} \times [\; -1 \quad -1 \quad +1 \quad -1\;]$$

---

[3]Strictly speaking, the connection weight between two cells representing two features is proportional to the *sum of the cross-products* between these two features. When the expected value (i.e., the mean) of each feature is 0, the sum of the cross-products becomes the covariance.

$$= \begin{bmatrix} +2 & +2 & 0 & 0 \\ +2 & +2 & 0 & 0 \\ 0 & 0 & +2 & -2 \\ 0 & 0 & -2 & +2 \end{bmatrix}$$

and so on up to *Step 10*, in which the 10th face is stored in addition to the first nine faces:

$$\mathbf{W}_{[10]} = \mathbf{W}_{[9]} + \mathbf{x}_{10}\mathbf{x}_{10}^T = \begin{bmatrix} +10 & +2 & +2 & +6 \\ +2 & +10 & +2 & -2 \\ +2 & +2 & +10 & -2 \\ +6 & -2 & -2 & +10 \end{bmatrix} .$$

We now have the complete connection matrix $\mathbf{W}$ (note that $\mathbf{W}$ could have been obtained directly from the stimulus matrix, as $\mathbf{W} = \mathbf{X}\mathbf{X}^T$). This matrix represents the pattern of connectivity of the autoassociative memory as illustrated by Fig. 3.6. Examination of this figure shows that the connection weights between cells 1 and 2, cells 1 and 3, and cells 2 and 3 have a value of "2." This reflects the fact that the values of the features corresponding to these cells are the same (either $+1$ and $+1$, or -1 and -1) in six faces but differ in four faces $[6 \times (+1) + 4 \times (-1) = 2]$. Similarly, the connection weight between cells 1 and 4 has a value of "6," indicating that the values of features 1 and 4 are the same in eight faces but differ in two faces $[8 \times (+1) + 2 \times (-1) = 6]$. Finally, the connection weights between cells 2 and 4, and cells 3 and 4 have a value of "-2," which indicates that the values of the features corresponding to these cells are the same only for four faces, and differ for six faces $[4 \times (+1) + 6 \times (-1) = -2]$.

In summary, the matrix of connections obtained with Hebbian learning captures the *regularities* or the *statistical structure* of the set of faces. These covariations or regularities constitute the "knowledge" of the memory and may be used as a basis for reconstructing partially ablated stimuli. For example, if a face is presented as a memory cue with Feature 4 set to zero (i.e., without indication for the mouth, as illustrated in Fig. 3.7a and 3.7b), the memory can use the pattern of connectivity of its weight matrix to fill in the missing information. Specifically, because the connection weight between Features 4 and 1 (6) is stronger than the connection weights between Features 4 and 2 as well as 4 and 3 (-2 and -2, respectively), Feature 4 will be given the same value as Feature 1. If Feature 1 is equal to $+1$ (*cf.* Fig. 3.7a), Feature 4 will be set to $+1$, as illustrated in Fig. 3.7a'. In contrast, if Feature 1 is equal to -1 (*cf.* Fig. 3.7b), Feature 4 will be set to -1, as illustrated in Fig. 3.7b'.

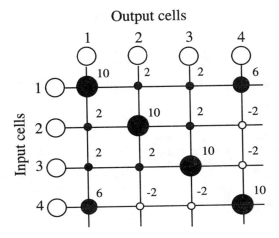

Figure 3.6: Connectivity pattern of an autoassociative memory trained to reconstruct the set of faces presented in Fig. 3.4. The magnitude of the synaptic weight is represented by the area of the circles and their sign by the color of the circles (black circles represent positive values, white circles negative values).

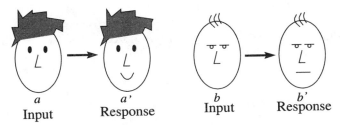

Figure 3.7: Example of partially ablated stimuli (a and b) and the response of the memory to these stimuli (a' and b').

3.5 Retrieval of a Learned Pattern

Retrieval of the kth pattern from the memory is performed by pre-multiplying the stimulus vector x_k by the weight matrix $\mathbf{W}$:

$$\widehat{\mathbf{x}}_k = \mathbf{W} \mathbf{x}_k \, , \qquad (3.6)$$

where $\widehat{\mathbf{x}}_k$ represents the memory response. The quality of this response is generally estimated by computing the cosine between the original vector, $\mathbf{x}_k$, and the memory response, $\widehat{\mathbf{x}}_k$:

$$\cos(\widehat{\mathbf{x}}_k, \mathbf{x}_k) = \frac{\widehat{\mathbf{x}}_k^T \mathbf{x}_k}{\|\widehat{\mathbf{x}}_k\| \, \|\mathbf{x}_k\|} , \tag{3.7}$$

where $\|\mathbf{x}_k\|$ and $\|\widehat{\mathbf{x}}_k\|$ are the respective Euclidean norms of $\mathbf{x}_k$ and $\widehat{\mathbf{x}}_k$ (i.e., $\|\mathbf{x}_k\| = \sqrt{\mathbf{x}_k^T \mathbf{x}_k}$). The cosine between the two vectors expresses the similarity between the stimulus learned by the memory and its reconstruction. A cosine of 1 indicates a perfect reconstruction. For example, retrieval of the first face of Fig. 3.4 is obtained by premultiplying the vector $\mathbf{x}_1$ by the weight matrix $\mathbf{W}$:

$$\widehat{\mathbf{x}}_1 = \mathbf{W}\mathbf{x}_1 = \begin{bmatrix} 10 & 2 & 2 & 6 \\ 2 & 10 & 2 & -2 \\ 2 & 2 & 10 & -2 \\ 6 & -2 & -2 & 10 \end{bmatrix} \times \begin{bmatrix} 1 \\ 1 \\ 1 \\ -1 \end{bmatrix}$$

$$= \begin{bmatrix} 10 \times 1 + 2 \times 1 + 2 \times 1 + 6 \times -1 \\ 2 \times 1 + 10 \times 1 + 2 \times 1 - 2 \times -1 \\ 2 \times 1 + 2 \times 1 + 10 \times 1 - 2 \times -1 \\ 6 \times 1 - 2 \times 1 - 2 \times 1 + 10 \times -1 \end{bmatrix} = \begin{bmatrix} 8 \\ 16 \\ 16 \\ -8 \end{bmatrix} = 8 \times \begin{bmatrix} 1 \\ 2 \\ 2 \\ -1 \end{bmatrix} .$$

Note that, although the general shape (i.e., patterns of $+$ and $-$) of the vector reconstructed from the memory is similar to that of the learned pattern, some differences exist and this face would be somewhat distorted. A more precise estimation of the quality of this response can be obtained by computing the cosine between the memory response and the original face: $\cos(\widehat{\mathbf{x}}_1, \mathbf{x}_1) = \frac{\widehat{\mathbf{x}}_1^T \mathbf{x}_1}{\|\widehat{\mathbf{x}}_1\| \, \|\mathbf{x}_1\|}$. The scalar product of $\widehat{\mathbf{x}}_1$ and $\mathbf{x}_1$ is obtained as

$$\widehat{\mathbf{x}}_1^T \mathbf{x}_1 = \begin{bmatrix} 8 & 16 & 16 & -8 \end{bmatrix} \times \begin{bmatrix} 1 \\ 1 \\ 1 \\ -1 \end{bmatrix} = 8 + 16 + 16 + 8 = 48 ,$$

the norms of $\widehat{\mathbf{x}}_1$ and $\mathbf{x}_1$ are obtained as $\|\widehat{\mathbf{x}}_1\| = \sqrt{\widehat{\mathbf{x}}_1^T \widehat{\mathbf{x}}_1} = \sqrt{640} = 25.2982$ and $\|\mathbf{x}_1\| = \sqrt{\mathbf{x}_1^T \mathbf{x}_1} = \sqrt{4} = 2$. This gives a cosine of

$$\cos(\widehat{\mathbf{x}}_1, \mathbf{x}_1) = \frac{48}{25.2982 \times 2} = \frac{48}{50.5964} = .9487 . \tag{3.8}$$

This value indicates that, although recall is not perfect ($.9487 < 1$), it is still relatively good (i.e., the relative relationship between features is preserved, positive features are still positive, and negative features are still negative). We shall see in Section 3.8 on page 36 that other methods can also be used to evaluate performance.

The complete set of faces can be recalled from the memory in a single step by premultiplying the face matrix $\mathbf{X}$ by the connection matrix $\mathbf{W}$:

$$\hat{\mathbf{X}} = \mathbf{WX} = \begin{bmatrix} 10 & 2 & 2 & 6 \\ 2 & 10 & 2 & -2 \\ 2 & 2 & 10 & -2 \\ 6 & -2 & -2 & 10 \end{bmatrix}$$

$$\times \begin{bmatrix} 1 & -1 & -1 & 1 & -1 & 1 & 1 & -1 & -1 & 1 \\ 1 & -1 & -1 & -1 & 1 & -1 & 1 & -1 & 1 & 1 \\ 1 & 1 & -1 & -1 & -1 & 1 & 1 & -1 & 1 & -1 \\ -1 & -1 & -1 & 1 & -1 & 1 & 1 & 1 & -1 & 1 \end{bmatrix}$$

$$= \begin{bmatrix} 8 & -16 & -20 & 12 & -16 & 16 & 20 & -8 & -12 & 16 \\ 16 & -8 & -12 & -12 & 8 & -8 & 12 & -16 & 12 & 8 \\ 16 & 8 & -12 & -12 & -8 & 8 & 12 & -16 & 12 & -8 \\ -8 & -16 & -12 & 20 & -16 & 16 & 12 & 8 & -20 & 16 \end{bmatrix},$$

where the first column is the reconstruction of Face 1, the second column the reconstruction of Face 2, and so on.

3.6 Limitations of Hebbian Learning

In the previous section we have seen how to recall a pattern from an autoassociative memory trained with Hebbian learning. In this section we analyze the performance of Hebbian learning using two different examples: one with perfect recall and one with imperfect recall.

3.6.1 Example 1: Perfect Recall

Suppose you want to store the third and fourth faces of Fig. 3.4 in an autoassociative memory $\mathbf{W}$ using Hebbian learning. These faces are represented by the vectors

$$\mathbf{x}_3 = \begin{bmatrix} -1 \\ -1 \\ -1 \\ -1 \end{bmatrix} \text{ and } \mathbf{x}_4 = \begin{bmatrix} +1 \\ -1 \\ -1 \\ +1 \end{bmatrix}, \text{ or by the matrix } \mathbf{X} = \begin{bmatrix} -1 & 1 \\ -1 & -1 \\ -1 & -1 \\ -1 & 1 \end{bmatrix}.$$

The autoassociative memory $\mathbf{W}$ is obtained as

$$\mathbf{W} = \mathbf{X}\mathbf{X}^T = \begin{bmatrix} -1 & 1 \\ -1 & -1 \\ -1 & -1 \\ -1 & 1 \end{bmatrix} \times \begin{bmatrix} -1 & -1 & -1 & -1 \\ 1 & -1 & -1 & 1 \end{bmatrix} = \begin{bmatrix} 2 & 0 & 0 & 2 \\ 0 & 2 & 2 & 0 \\ 0 & 2 & 2 & 0 \\ 2 & 0 & 0 & 2 \end{bmatrix}.$$

$$(3.9)$$

Recall of the two faces is obtained by premultiplying the face matrix $\mathbf{X}$ by the weight matrix $\mathbf{W}$, as follows:

$$\widehat{\mathbf{X}} = \mathbf{W}\mathbf{X} = \begin{bmatrix} 2 & 0 & 0 & 2 \\ 0 & 2 & 2 & 0 \\ 0 & 2 & 2 & 0 \\ 2 & 0 & 0 & 2 \end{bmatrix} \times \begin{bmatrix} -1 & 1 \\ -1 & -1 \\ -1 & -1 \\ -1 & 1 \end{bmatrix} = \begin{bmatrix} -4 & 4 \\ -4 & -4 \\ -4 & -4 \\ -4 & 4 \end{bmatrix} = 4 \times \mathbf{X}.$$

This result indicates that, when prompted with the faces it has learned, the memory gives them back amplified (i.e., multiplied) by a factor of 4. As a consequence, the cosine between the original and the recalled faces is one.

3.6.2 Example 2: Imperfect Recall

Now, suppose that you want to store Faces 2 and 4 in a memory using Hebbian learning. These faces are represented by the vectors

$$\mathbf{x}_2 = \begin{bmatrix} -1 \\ -1 \\ +1 \\ -1 \end{bmatrix} \text{ and } \mathbf{x}_4 = \begin{bmatrix} +1 \\ -1 \\ -1 \\ +1 \end{bmatrix}, \text{ or by the matrix } \mathbf{X} = \begin{bmatrix} -1 & 1 \\ -1 & -1 \\ 1 & -1 \\ -1 & 1 \end{bmatrix}.$$

The weight matrix $\mathbf{W}$ is obtained as

$$\mathbf{W} = \mathbf{X}\mathbf{X}^T = \begin{bmatrix} -1 & 1 \\ -1 & -1 \\ 1 & -1 \\ -1 & 1 \end{bmatrix} \times \begin{bmatrix} -1 & -1 & 1 & -1 \\ 1 & -1 & -1 & 1 \end{bmatrix} = \begin{bmatrix} 2 & 0 & -2 & 2 \\ 0 & 2 & 0 & 0 \\ -2 & 0 & 2 & -2 \\ 2 & 0 & -2 & 2 \end{bmatrix}$$

and recall as

$$\widehat{\mathbf{X}} = \mathbf{W}\mathbf{X} = \begin{bmatrix} 2 & 0 & -2 & 2 \\ 0 & 2 & 0 & 0 \\ -2 & 0 & 2 & -2 \\ 2 & 0 & -2 & 2 \end{bmatrix} \times \begin{bmatrix} -1 & 1 \\ -1 & -1 \\ 1 & -1 \\ -1 & 1 \end{bmatrix} = \begin{bmatrix} -6 & 6 \\ -2 & -2 \\ 6 & -6 \\ -6 & 6 \end{bmatrix}.$$

$$(3.10)$$

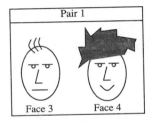 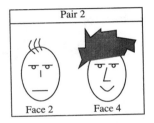

Figure 3.8: The two pairs of faces used to illustrate the limitation of Hebbian learning. Pair 1: 2 orthogonal stimuli; Pair 2: 2 non-orthogonal stimuli.

Now the memory does not give back the faces it has learned. This is confirmed by computing the cosines between the original face vectors and their reconstructions:

$$\cos(\widehat{x}_2, x_2) = \frac{\widehat{x}_2^T x_2}{\|\widehat{x}_2\| \|x_2\|} = \frac{20}{\sqrt{112}\sqrt{4}} = \frac{20}{10.5830 \times 2} = .9449$$

$$\cos(\widehat{x}_4, x_4) = \frac{\widehat{x}_4^T x_4}{\|\widehat{x}_4\| \|x_4\|} = \frac{20}{\sqrt{112}\sqrt{4}} = \frac{20}{10.5830 \times 2} = .9449.$$
(3.11)

3.6.3 Performance Analysis

So far, we have shown that, in some cases, the memory recalls perfectly the patterns it has learned, but in other cases the learned patterns are somewhat distorted. But when is performance perfect, and when is it not? To answer this question, we can compare the first pair of faces (Fig. 3.8, left panel) stored in the memory with the second pair (Fig. 3.8, right panel). Starting with the perfectly recalled pair,

$$x_3^T = [-1 \quad -1 \quad -1 \quad -1] \quad , \quad x_4^T = [+1 \quad -1 \quad -1 \quad +1],$$

we see that the two faces have two features in common (nose and eyes) and two different features (hair and mouth). Equivalently, we can say that the two faces have as many similar features as they have different features. Hence, knowing the value of a given feature of one face does not give any information about the value of the same feature for the other face (i.e., the probability of the two features being similar is equal to their probability of being different). More formally, we say that the vectors representing the two faces are *uncorrelated*, or *orthogonal*. This is equivalent to saying that their scalar product is equal to zero:

$$x_3^T x_4 = [-1 \quad -1 \quad -1 \quad -1] \begin{bmatrix} +1 \\ -1 \\ -1 \\ +1 \end{bmatrix} = 0 \,.$$

Examining the second pair of faces (not perfectly reconstructed)

$$x_2^T = [-1 \quad -1 \quad +1 \quad -1] \quad , \quad x_4^T = [+1 \quad -1 \quad -1 \quad +1] \,,$$

we see that Faces 2 and 4 have only one feature in common (the eyes) and differ for the three other features. Hence, in this case, if we know the value of a given feature of a face, we can bet that the corresponding feature of the other face will tend to have the opposite value (because the probability of two features being different is greater than their probability of being similar: .75 as opposed to .25). Formally, we say that the two vectors are *correlated*, or *not orthogonal*. In brief, their scalar product is not zero:

$$x_2^T x_4 = [-1 \quad -1 \quad +1 \quad -1] \begin{bmatrix} +1 \\ -1 \\ -1 \\ +1 \end{bmatrix} = -2 \,.$$

In summary, we have illustrated that when the input vectors stored in the memory are mutually (pairwise) orthogonal, recall of a learned pattern is perfect. When the input vectors are not orthogonal, the memory adds noise (or crosstalk) to the original pattern. This is shown by developing the formula for recall of the learned pattern x_ℓ:

$$\hat{x}_\ell = W x_\ell = \sum_k x_k x_k^T x_\ell$$

$$= \sum_k (x_k^T x_\ell) x_k = (x_\ell^T x_\ell) x_\ell + \sum_{k \neq \ell} (x_k^T x_\ell) x_k \qquad (3.12)$$

where the term $\sum_{k \neq \ell} (x_k^T x_\ell) x_k$ represents the interference or crosstalk between the pattern presented as input and the stored patterns. When all the patterns in the input set are mutually orthogonal, the scalar products between each vector x_k and the test vector x_ℓ are equal to zero and therefore $\sum_{k \neq \ell} (x_k^T x_\ell) x_k = 0$ and the response of the memory to pattern x_ℓ is the pattern itself scaled by (i.e., multiplied by) its scalar product: $\hat{x}_\ell = (x_\ell^T x_\ell) x_\ell$. If the input patterns are normalized[4] so that their length is equal to 1 (i.e., $\|\mathbf{x}_k\| = 1$), the response of the memory is the input pattern.

When the patterns in the input set are *not* mutually orthogonal, the scalar products between each vector $\mathbf{x}_k$ and the test vector $\mathbf{x}_\ell$ are not equal to zero, and the response of the memory to pattern $\mathbf{x}_\ell$ is the pattern itself scaled by its scalar product, [i.e., the term $(\mathbf{x}_\ell^T \mathbf{x}_\ell)\mathbf{x}_\ell$] *plus* the interference component: $\sum_{k \neq \ell}(\mathbf{x}_k^T \mathbf{x}_\ell)\mathbf{x}_k$. Because the scalar product between two vectors increases as a function of their similarity, this interference component depends on the overall similarity between the test pattern and all the other stored patterns. The greater the similarity is, the greater the interference component, and therefore the more distorted the memory response.

3.7 Generalization to New Stimuli

In the previous sections, we have examined the ability of an auto-associative memory trained with Hebbian learning to retrieve or reconstruct a learned pattern. In this section we will look at what happens when a new pattern (i.e., one that has not been learned by the memory) is presented as a memory key. Technically we say that we are looking at the ability of the memory to *generalize* to new patterns.

Suppose you want to test the ability of the memory in which you have stored Faces 3 and 4 to reconstruct Face 1. The weight matrix is given by Eq. 3.9 on page 32. Recall of Face 1 is obtained as

$$\widehat{\mathbf{x}}_1 = \mathbf{W}\mathbf{x}_1 = \begin{bmatrix} 2 & 0 & 0 & 2 \\ 0 & 2 & 2 & 0 \\ 0 & 2 & 2 & 0 \\ 2 & 0 & 0 & 2 \end{bmatrix} \times \begin{bmatrix} +1 \\ +1 \\ +1 \\ -1 \end{bmatrix} = \begin{bmatrix} 0 \\ 4 \\ 4 \\ 0 \end{bmatrix}.$$

The quality of the response of the memory can be estimated by computing the cosine between $\widehat{\mathbf{x}}_1$ and $\mathbf{x}_1$:

$$\cos(\widehat{\mathbf{x}}_1, \mathbf{x}_1) = \frac{8}{\sqrt{32}\sqrt{4}} = \frac{8}{5.6569 \times 2} = .7071 ,$$

which is smaller than the cosine of 1 obtained with a learned pattern (see page 32). Suppose now that you want to test the ability of the memory in which you have stored Faces 2 and 4 to reconstruct Face 1. The weight matrix is given by Eq. 3.10 on page 32. Recall of Face 1 is

---

[4]This is achieved by dividing each element of the vector by the original norm of the vector.

now obtained as

$$\widehat{\mathbf{x}}_1 = \mathbf{W}\mathbf{x}_1 = \begin{bmatrix} 2 & 0 & -2 & 2 \\ 0 & 2 & 0 & 0 \\ -2 & 0 & 2 & -2 \\ 2 & 0 & -2 & 2 \end{bmatrix} \times \begin{bmatrix} +1 \\ +1 \\ +1 \\ -1 \end{bmatrix} = \begin{bmatrix} -2 \\ +2 \\ +2 \\ -2 \end{bmatrix} .$$

The quality of this response is estimated by

$$\cos(\widehat{\mathbf{x}}_1, \mathbf{x}_1) = \frac{4}{\sqrt{16}\sqrt{4}} = \frac{4}{4 \times 2} = .50 ,$$

which again is smaller than the cosine of .9449 obtained for the learned faces (see page 33). Comparing the quality of reconstruction of Face 1 by the two memories indicates that the first memory is better able to generalize to this new face than the second memory (.71 vs. .50).

The fact that an autoassociative memory is better able to reconstruct learned patterns than new patterns is generally interpreted as an indication that the memory is able to *discriminate* between learned and new patterns or to *recognize* learned patterns. More precisely, the memory is said to recognize learned patterns if, on the average, the cosines between reconstructed and learned patterns are larger than the cosines between reconstructed and new patterns.

3.8 Reconstruction Error, Error Term, and Global Error

We have seen in Section 3.5 on page 29 that a first way of evaluating the performance of an autoassociator is to compute the cosine between each pattern stored and its reconstruction. A second way of evaluating the quality of the recall of a pattern is to compute the *reconstruction error* for this pattern. The reconstruction error is defined as the difference between a perfect performance and the actual performance of the system (as measured by the cosine between target and output). Formally, the reconstruction error for the kth pattern is noted e_k and computed as

$$e_k = 1 - \cos(\widehat{\mathbf{x}}_k, \mathbf{x}_k) . \tag{3.13}$$

For example, the reconstruction error of Face 1 (see Eq. 3.8 on page 30) is $e_1 = 1 - .9487 = .0513$. It is also sometimes convenient to evaluate the *global* performance of a system in terms of the error. We define the *global error*, denoted $\mathcal{E}$, as the sum of the reconstruction error of all stored patterns ($\mathcal{E} = \sum e_k$).

A third way, yet, to measure the quality of the answer, which we will use in the section on Widrow-Hoff learning, is the *error term vector*. The error term vector, denoted e_k, is defined as the difference between the target and the response [i.e., $e_k = (x_k - \widehat{x}_k)$]. For example, the error term vector when recalling Face 1 is

$$e_1^T = \begin{bmatrix} 1 & 1 & 1 & -1 \end{bmatrix} - \begin{bmatrix} 8 & 16 & 16 & -8 \end{bmatrix} = \begin{bmatrix} -7 & -15 & -15 & 7 \end{bmatrix}.$$

The matrix $\mathbf{E}$ represents the error term vectors for all patterns.

An alternative approach for expressing the reconstruction error is to use the *reconstruction error function* for pattern k, defined as: $\mathcal{J}_k = \frac{1}{2}e_k^T e_k = \frac{1}{2}(x_k - \widehat{x}_k)^T(x_k - \widehat{x}_k)$ [*cf.* Section 3.11 on page 45]. If input and output vectors are normalized, then the reconstruction error and the reconstruction error function are equal. The *global error function* is the sum of the error reconstruction functions for all patterns. It is denoted $\mathcal{J}$. It is equal to

$$\mathcal{J} = \sum_k \mathcal{J}_k = \frac{1}{2}\sum_k (x_k - \widehat{x}_k)^T(x_k - \widehat{x}_k)$$
$$= \frac{1}{2}\text{trace}\left\{(\mathbf{X} - \mathbf{WX})^T(\mathbf{X} - \mathbf{WX})\right\} \tag{3.14}$$

(with the trace of a matrix being the sum of its diagonal elements).

3.9 The Widrow-Hoff Learning Rule

We have seen that, when learned patterns are not orthogonal, Hebbian learning is imperfect: There is some difference or error between a stimulus and its reconstruction. The performance of the memory can be improved by using the Widrow-Hoff learning rule presented in Chapter 2. The Widrow-Hoff algorithm adjusts iteratively the weights of the connection matrix in order to maximize the quality of reconstruction of the input patterns. First, the values of the weights are initialized. This can be achieved using Hebbian learning or by setting them to some random or fixed value (i.e., zero). Then a learned pattern (randomly chosen) is presented as input to the memory and the difference between the pattern and the response of the memory is computed. This difference is called the "error term" or simply the "error" (see page 36). If the reconstruction error is equal to zero, then no weight correction is made (because recall is perfect) and another pattern is chosen. If the reconstruction error is not zero, then the values of the weights are adjusted by multiplying the error vector by the input vector, and a new randomly chosen pattern is presented as a memory key. This procedure is repeated across the set of patterns to be learned. Smaller and smaller adjustments are made over time until the global error is equal to zero and all the patterns are perfectly reconstructed. The main idea is as follows:

> With Widrow-Hoff learning, the connection weight between two neurons is iteratively adjusted in order to have a smaller error term for a second presentation of the same stimulus.

Formally, the weight matrix at iteration $n + 1$ is expressed as

$$\mathbf{W}_{[n+1]} = \mathbf{W}_{[n]} + \eta(\mathbf{x}_k - \mathbf{W}_{[n]}\mathbf{x}_k)\mathbf{x}_k^T = \mathbf{W}_{[n]} + \eta(\mathbf{x}_k - \widehat{\mathbf{x}}_k)\mathbf{x}_k^T$$
$$= \mathbf{W}_{[n]} + \eta\mathbf{e}\mathbf{x}_k^T = \mathbf{W}_{[n]} + \mathbf{\Delta}_{\mathbf{W}_{[n]}}, \qquad (3.15)$$

where n represents the iteration number, η ("eta") is a small positive constant, $\mathbf{e}$ is the error vector, $\mathbf{\Delta}_{\mathbf{W}_{[n]}}$ is the matrix of corrections for $\mathbf{W}$ at the nth iteration, and k is randomly chosen.

The correction applied to the weight matrix will give a smaller global error when the same stimulus is presented again. Because the error diminishes at each iteration, this type of technique is called a *gradient descent algorithm* in numerical analysis (see Section 3.11, page 45*ff.*). As for Hebbian learning, this algorithm can be expressed in a more practical way by using the stimulus matrix. In this case, the error is computed for the complete set of patterns before implementing the correction. This is generally called "*batch* learning" as opposed to "*single stimulus* learning" (described by Eq. 3.15). In the case of a linear autoassociative memory, the two types of learning converge to the same solution. Batch learning, however, usually converges to the correct solution faster than single stimulus learning. For batch learning, the weight matrix at iteration $n + 1$ is expressed as

$$\mathbf{W}_{[n+1]} = \mathbf{W}_{[n]} + \eta(\mathbf{X} - \mathbf{W}_{[n]}\mathbf{X})\mathbf{X}^T = \mathbf{W}_{[n]} + \eta(\mathbf{X} - \widehat{\mathbf{X}})\mathbf{X}^T$$
$$= \mathbf{W}_{[n]} + \eta\mathbf{E}\mathbf{X}_k^T = \mathbf{W}_{[n]} + \mathbf{\Delta}_{\mathbf{W}_{[n]}}, \qquad (3.16)$$

where $\mathbf{E}$ represents the error matrix and $\mathbf{\Delta}_{\mathbf{W}_{[n]}}$ the matrix of corrections for $\mathbf{W}$ at the nth iteration.

3.9.1 Back to the Numerical Example

Earlier we saw that Hebbian learning suffered from crosstalk when trying to store Faces 2 and 4 of Fig. 3.4, because they were not orthogonal. Here we see that the non-orthogonality of these two faces is no longer a problem when the Widrow-Hoff learning algorithm is used to create the weight matrix. Remember that Faces 2 and 4 are represented by the matrix

$$\mathbf{X} = \begin{bmatrix} -1 & 1 \\ -1 & -1 \\ 1 & -1 \\ -1 & 1 \end{bmatrix} .$$

The first step in using the Widrow-Hoff algorithm is to decide upon a value for the learning constant η. As we shall see at the end of this section, this decision is far from being trivial. However, for now let us decide upon the value .2. The next step is to initialize the matrix $\mathbf{W}$. For clarity, we initialize it to zeros:

$$\mathbf{W}_{[0]} = \begin{bmatrix} 0 & 0 & 0 & 0 \\ 0 & 0 & 0 & 0 \\ 0 & 0 & 0 & 0 \\ 0 & 0 & 0 & 0 \end{bmatrix} .$$

We are now ready to start the iterations described in Eq. 3.16.

3.9.1.1 Iteration 1:

Step 1: Recall the faces

$$\widehat{\mathbf{X}}_{[0]} = \mathbf{W}_{[0]} \mathbf{X} = \begin{bmatrix} 0 & 0 & 0 & 0 \\ 0 & 0 & 0 & 0 \\ 0 & 0 & 0 & 0 \\ 0 & 0 & 0 & 0 \end{bmatrix} \times \begin{bmatrix} -1 & 1 \\ -1 & -1 \\ 1 & -1 \\ -1 & 1 \end{bmatrix} = \begin{bmatrix} 0 & 0 \\ 0 & 0 \\ 0 & 0 \\ 0 & 0 \end{bmatrix}$$

Step 2: Compute the error

$$\mathbf{E}_{[0]} = \mathbf{X} - \widehat{\mathbf{X}}_{[0]} = \begin{bmatrix} -1 & 1 \\ -1 & -1 \\ 1 & -1 \\ -1 & 1 \end{bmatrix} - \begin{bmatrix} 0 & 0 \\ 0 & 0 \\ 0 & 0 \\ 0 & 0 \end{bmatrix} = \begin{bmatrix} -1 & 1 \\ -1 & -1 \\ 1 & -1 \\ -1 & 1 \end{bmatrix}$$

Step 3: Compute the matrix of correction

$$\mathbf{\Delta w}_{[0]} = .2 \times \mathbf{E}_{[0]} \mathbf{X}^T = .2 \times \begin{bmatrix} -1 & 1 \\ -1 & -1 \\ 1 & -1 \\ -1 & 1 \end{bmatrix} \times \begin{bmatrix} -1 & -1 & 1 & -1 \\ 1 & -1 & -1 & 1 \end{bmatrix}$$

$$= \begin{bmatrix} .4 & 0 & -.4 & .4 \\ 0 & .4 & 0 & 0 \\ -.4 & 0 & .4 & -.4 \\ .4 & 0 & -.4 & .4 \end{bmatrix}$$

Step 4: Update the weight matrix

$$\mathbf{W}_{[1]} = \mathbf{W}_{[0]} + \boldsymbol{\Delta}\mathbf{w}_{[0]} = \begin{bmatrix} 0 & 0 & 0 & 0 \\ 0 & 0 & 0 & 0 \\ 0 & 0 & 0 & 0 \\ 0 & 0 & 0 & 0 \end{bmatrix} + \begin{bmatrix} .4 & 0 & -.4 & .4 \\ 0 & .4 & 0 & 0 \\ -.4 & 0 & .4 & -.4 \\ .4 & 0 & -.4 & .4 \end{bmatrix}$$

$$= \begin{bmatrix} .4 & 0 & -.4 & .4 \\ 0 & .4 & 0 & .0 \\ -.4 & 0 & .4 & -.4 \\ .4 & 0 & -.4 & .4 \end{bmatrix} \quad \ldots \text{ and so on up to}$$

3.9.1.2 Iteration 24:

$$\widehat{\mathbf{X}}_{[23]} = \mathbf{W}_{[23]}\mathbf{X} = \begin{bmatrix} .333 & 0 & -.333 & .333 \\ 0 & 1.00 & 0 & 0 \\ -.333 & 0 & .333 & -.333 \\ .333 & 0 & -.333 & .333 \end{bmatrix} \times \begin{bmatrix} -1 & 1 \\ -1 & -1 \\ 1 & -1 \\ -1 & 1 \end{bmatrix}$$

$$= \begin{bmatrix} -1 & 1 \\ -1 & -1 \\ 1 & -1 \\ -1 & 1 \end{bmatrix}$$

$$\mathbf{E}_{[23]} = \widehat{\mathbf{X}}_{[23]} - \mathbf{X} = \begin{bmatrix} -1 & 1 \\ -1 & -1 \\ 1 & -1 \\ -1 & 1 \end{bmatrix} - \begin{bmatrix} -1 & 1 \\ -1 & -1 \\ 1 & -1 \\ -1 & 1 \end{bmatrix} = \begin{bmatrix} 0 & 0 \\ 0 & 0 \\ 0 & 0 \\ 0 & 0 \end{bmatrix}$$

$$\boldsymbol{\Delta}\mathbf{w}_{[23]} = .2 \times \mathbf{E}_{[23]}\mathbf{X}^T$$

$$= .2 \times \begin{bmatrix} 0 & 0 \\ 0 & 0 \\ 0 & 0 \\ 0 & 0 \end{bmatrix} \times \begin{bmatrix} -1 & -1 & 1 & -1 \\ 1 & -1 & -1 & 1 \end{bmatrix} = \begin{bmatrix} 0 & 0 & 0 & 0 & 0 \\ 0 & 0 & 0 & 0 & 0 \\ 0 & 0 & 0 & 0 & 0 \\ 0 & 0 & 0 & 0 & 0 \end{bmatrix}$$

et voilà! The Widrow-Hoff algorithm converged to the correct solution in 24 iterations. It is important to note, however, that the number of iterations necessary to reach convergence depends on the value chosen for the learning constant.

Setting the value for the learning constant is somewhat delicate. If η is too small, the algorithm will take a large number of iterations to converge to the correct answer. But if η is too large, the memory could oscillate around the correct answer (going indefinitely from slightly greater to slightly smaller) or could even "explode" (in the jargon of computer scientists) by going further and further away from the correct solution. We will show in the next section that it is possible both to find a value of η that guarantees convergence and to implement the Widrow-Hoff algorithm more simply by using the eigendecomposition of $\mathbf{W}$.

3.10 Eigen and Singular Value Decompositions: PCA

The inner working of the linear autoassociator is closely related to the *eigen* or *spectral* decomposition of a square matrix into eigenvectors and eigenvalues and to the more general *singular value* decomposition of a rectangular matrix. These techniques decompose a matrix into a weighted sum of simple matrices (by "simple matrix," we mean a matrix obtained by multiplication of a column vector by a row vector, also called a "rank one" matrix). Within a statistical framework, these decompositions give rise to *principal component analysis* (PCA), which explains why the linear autoassociator is sometimes called a principal components neural network.

3.10.1 Eigenvectors and Eigenvalues

Eigenvectors exist only for square matrices. An eigenvector of a square matrix has the defining property that multiplication by this matrix is equivalent to multiplication by a scalar (i.e., the *length* of the vector changes, its *direction* does not[5]). Formally, if $\mathbf{u}$ is an eigenvector of $\mathbf{W}$,

$$\mathbf{W}\mathbf{u} = \lambda\mathbf{u}, \qquad (3.17)$$

where λ (the Greek letter "lambda") is a scalar called the *eigenvalue* associated with the eigenvector $\mathbf{u}$. This scalar indicates how much the length of $\mathbf{u}$ is changed when multiplied by $\mathbf{W}$. In general there are several eigenvectors for a given matrix (some of them may have the same eigenvalue). The number of eigenvectors, with a nonzero eigenvalue, of a matrix is equal to its *rank*[6] (which is always less than or equal to I, the number of rows and columns of $\mathbf{W}$). For exam-

---

[5]In general, multiplication by a square matrix changes *both* the length and magnitude of a vector.
[6]The rank of a matrix is the number of linearly independent rows or columns of this matrix.

ple, the vector $\mathbf{u} = \begin{bmatrix} 1 \\ 1 \end{bmatrix}^T$ is an eigenvector of $\mathbf{W} = \begin{bmatrix} 1 & .5 \\ .5 & 1 \end{bmatrix}$, with eigenvalue $\lambda = 1.5$, because

$$\mathbf{Wu} = \begin{bmatrix} 1 & .5 \\ .5 & 1 \end{bmatrix} \times \begin{bmatrix} 1 \\ 1 \end{bmatrix} = \begin{bmatrix} 1.5 \\ 1.5 \end{bmatrix} = 1.5 \times \mathbf{u} = \lambda \mathbf{u}. \tag{3.18}$$

Traditionally, the set of eigenvectors of a given matrix is represented by a matrix $\mathbf{U}$ in which the first column represents the eigenvector with the largest eigenvalue, the second column the eigenvector with the second largest eigenvalue, and so on. The corresponding eigenvalues are represented by a diagonal matrix $\mathbf{\Lambda}$ (the Greek uppercase letter "Lambda") in which the elements on the diagonal are the eigenvalues and all the other values are zeros. Using this notation, Eq. 3.17 can be rewritten as $\mathbf{WU} = \mathbf{\Lambda U}$, and the matrix $\mathbf{W}$ can be expressed as a function of its eigenvectors and eigenvalues as

$$\mathbf{W} = \mathbf{U \Lambda U}^{-1}, \tag{3.19}$$

where $\mathbf{U}^{-1}$ is the inverse of $\mathbf{U}$ (i.e., $\mathbf{U}^{-1}\mathbf{U} = \mathbf{UU}^{-1} = \mathbf{I}$, with $\mathbf{I}$ being the identity matrix). In the particular case when $\mathbf{W}$ is symmetric and can be obtained as the product of a matrix by its transpose, the eigenvalues of $\mathbf{W}$ are all positive or zeros and its eigenvectors are pairwise orthogonal ($\mathbf{W}$ is said to be *positive semi-definite*). In this particular case, if the eigenvectors are normalized (i.e., their length is one), then $\mathbf{U}^{-1} = \mathbf{U}^T$, (i.e., $\mathbf{U}^T\mathbf{U} = \mathbf{I}$) and Eq. 3.19 simplifies to $\mathbf{W} = \mathbf{U \Lambda U}^T = \sum_\ell \lambda_\ell \mathbf{u}_\ell \mathbf{u}_\ell^T$ (i.e., the matrices $\mathbf{u}_\ell \mathbf{u}_\ell^T$ are the rank one matrices used to build back $\mathbf{W}$, and the λ_ℓ are the weights).

In the PCA framework, the eigenvectors are called the *principal components* and the eigenvalues give the amount of *variance explained* by the components.

3.10.2 Singular Value Decomposition (SVD)

The notions of eigenvectors and eigenvalues of a positive semi-definite matrix can be used to define the more general *singular value decomposition* of a rectangular matrix. Specifically, any rectangular matrix, $\mathbf{X}$, can be expressed as

$$\mathbf{X} = \mathbf{U \Delta V}^T, \tag{3.20}$$

where $\mathbf{U}$ is the matrix of eigenvectors of $\mathbf{XX}^T$ ($\mathbf{XX}^T = \mathbf{U \Lambda U}^T$, with $\mathbf{U}^T\mathbf{U} = \mathbf{I}$); $\mathbf{V}$ is the matrix of eigenvectors of $\mathbf{X}^T\mathbf{X}$ ($\mathbf{X}^T\mathbf{X} =$

$\mathbf{V}\mathbf{\Lambda}\mathbf{V}^T$, with $\mathbf{V}^T\mathbf{V} = \mathbf{I}$); and $\mathbf{\Delta}$ (the Greek uppercase letter "Delta") is the diagonal matrix of singular values of $\mathbf{X}$. The singular values of $\mathbf{X}$ are equal to the square root of the eigenvalues of $\mathbf{X}\mathbf{X}^T$ and $\mathbf{X}^T\mathbf{X}$ (they are the same). Therefore $\mathbf{\Delta} = \mathbf{\Lambda}^{\frac{1}{2}}$.

3.10.3 Widrow-Hoff Learning and SVD

The eigendecomposition of $\mathbf{W}$ is a major tool to analyze the Widrow-Hoff learning rule. Specifically, Abdi, Valentin, O'Toole, and Edelman (1996, see also Widrow & Stearns, 1985) pointed out that the Widrow-Hoff equation

$$\mathbf{W}_{[n]} = \mathbf{W}_{[n-1]} + \eta(\mathbf{X} - \mathbf{W}_{[n-1]}\mathbf{X})\mathbf{X}^T \qquad (3.21)$$

can be expressed from the eigendecomposition of $\mathbf{W}$ as

$$\mathbf{W}_{[n]} = \mathbf{U}\mathbf{\Phi}_{[n]}\mathbf{U}^T \quad \text{with} \quad \mathbf{\Phi}_{[n]} = [\mathbf{I} - (\mathbf{I} - \eta\mathbf{\Lambda})^n], \qquad (3.22)$$

with $\mathbf{\Phi}_{[n]}$ (read "uppercase Phi of n") being the eigenvalue matrix at epoch n. This formulation shows that the Widrow-Hoff error correction rule affects only the eigenvalues of $\mathbf{W}$ (the eigenvectors are not changed by learning). More specifically, if λ_{max} (read "lambda max") denotes the largest eigenvalue of $\mathbf{W}$, it follows from Eq. 3.22 that when η is smaller than $2\lambda_{max}^{-1}$, using the Widrow-Hoff rule equalizes all the eigenvalues of $\mathbf{W}$ (all the eigenvalues converge to the value 1). It is assumed, of course, that only the eigenvectors with a nonzero eigenvalue are taken into account. In more technical terms, we say that the Widrow-Hoff rule *sphericizes* or *whitens* the weight matrix.[7] Hence, at convergence, $\mathbf{W}$ becomes $\mathbf{W}_{[\infty]} = \mathbf{U}\mathbf{U}^T$. For single stimulus mode learning, Eq. 3.22 gives the state of the matrix after the nth learning epoch (i.e., it supposes that all the patterns have been learned).

3.10.3.1 Back to a Numerical Example

As an illustration, we can use the singular value decomposition approach to reconstruct the weight matrix presented in the numerical

---

[7]The expression "to sphericize" comes from the interpretation of the eigenvalue of an eigenvector as its *length*. After Widrow-Hoff learning, all the eigenvectors have the same eigenvalue. Therefore, according to this interpretation, all the eigenvectors have the same length and the multidimensional space defined by these eigenvectors has the shape of a sphere (because in a sphere, all the diameters have the same length). To "whiten" comes from the signal processing approach, which identifies each eigenvector as a frequency component and each eigenvalue as its importance. Because white light is made of all frequencies with an equal importance, to equalize the eigenvalues "whitens" the signal.

example for the Widrow-Hoff rule (see page 38). Recall that our goal was to store the faces represented by the matrix

$$\mathbf{X} = \begin{bmatrix} -1 & +1 \\ -1 & -1 \\ +1 & -1 \\ -1 & +1 \end{bmatrix}.$$

The first step is to compute the singular value decomposition of $\mathbf{X}$:

$$\mathbf{X} = \mathbf{U}\boldsymbol{\Delta}\mathbf{V}^T$$

$$= \begin{bmatrix} .5774 & 0 \\ 0 & 1 \\ -.5774 & 0 \\ .5774 & 0 \end{bmatrix} \times \left\{ \begin{bmatrix} 2.4495 & 0 \\ 0 & 1.4142 \end{bmatrix} \right\} \times \begin{bmatrix} -.7071 & .7071 \\ -.7071 & -.7071 \end{bmatrix}.$$

Then we start reconstructing $\mathbf{W}$ using the value of $\eta = .2$ as before. *Iteration 1:* $\mathbf{W}_{[1]} = \mathbf{U}\boldsymbol{\Phi}_{[1]}\mathbf{U}^T$, with

$$\boldsymbol{\Phi}_{[1]} = \mathbf{I} - (\mathbf{I} - \eta\boldsymbol{\Lambda})^1 \quad \text{where} \quad \boldsymbol{\Lambda} = \boldsymbol{\Delta}^2 \text{ and } n = 1 \text{ (see Eq. 3.22)}$$

$$= \begin{bmatrix} 1 & 0 \\ 0 & 1 \end{bmatrix} - \left(\begin{bmatrix} 1 & 0 \\ 0 & 1 \end{bmatrix} - .2 \times \begin{bmatrix} 2.4495^2 & 0 \\ 0 & 1.4142^2 \end{bmatrix} \right)^1 = \begin{bmatrix} 1.2 & 0 \\ 0 & .4 \end{bmatrix},$$

which gives

$$\mathbf{W}_{[1]} = \begin{bmatrix} .5774 & 0 \\ 0 & 1 \\ -.5774 & 0 \\ .5774 & 0 \end{bmatrix} \times \begin{bmatrix} 1.2 & 0 \\ 0 & .4 \end{bmatrix} \times \begin{bmatrix} .5774 & 0 & -.5774 & .5774 \\ 0 & 1 & 0 & 0 \end{bmatrix}$$

$$= \begin{bmatrix} .4 & 0 & -.4 & .4 \\ 0 & .4 & 0 & 0 \\ -.4 & 0 & .4 & -.4 \\ .4 & 0 & -.4 & .4 \end{bmatrix} \quad \dots \text{ and so on up to}$$

$$\mathbf{W}_{[\infty]} = \mathbf{U}\mathbf{U}^T = \begin{bmatrix} .5774 & 0 \\ 0 & 1 \\ -.5774 & 0 \\ .5774 & 0 \end{bmatrix} \times \begin{bmatrix} .5774 & 0 & -.5774 & .5774 \\ 0 & 1 & 0 & 0 \end{bmatrix}$$

$$= \begin{bmatrix} .333 & 0 & -.333 & .333 \\ 0 & 1 & 0 & 0 \\ -.333 & 0 & .333 & -.333 \\ .333 & 0 & -.333 & .333 \end{bmatrix},$$

which corresponds to the value of $\mathbf{W}$ found in Section 3.9.1.2 on page 40. This example illustrates that creating a weight matrix from the eigenvectors of $\mathbf{XX}^T$ as $\mathbf{W}_{[\infty]} = \mathbf{UU}^T$ is equivalent to complete Widrow-Hoff learning.

3.11 The Widrow-Hoff Rule and Gradient Descent

The Widrow-Hoff learning rule can also be seen as an iterative algorithm whose goal is to find the minimum of an error function. In what follows we show that the Widrow-Hoff learning rule is implementing a classic technique of numerical analysis and optimization known as *the gradient descent method* (*cf.* Chong & Zak, 1996).

3.11.1 Gradient Descent

The gradient of a function is defined as the matrix of the first derivative of that function. Suppose that you want to minimize (i.e., to locate the minimum of) the function $y = g(\mathbf{W})$ and that the parameters of this function are stored in a matrix denoted $\mathbf{W}$. The gradient descent algorithm proceeds as follows.

1. Choose the initial values of $\mathbf{W}_{[0]}$. In general, these values are chosen randomly, but a first good guess can also be used if any can be made.

2. Compute the local gradient of g denoted by ∇_g (read "grad g," or also "nabla g," even "Del g"), as the partial derivative of g with respect to $\mathbf{W}_{[n]}$ (∂ is read "partial"): $\dfrac{\partial g(\mathbf{W}_{[n]})}{\partial \mathbf{W}_{[n]}} = \nabla_g$.

3. Change the values of $\mathbf{W}_{[n]}$ in the inverse direction of its gradient (because the gradient indicates the direction in which the function increases, the inverse direction indicates the direction of a possible minimum). Formally, the correction to apply to $\mathbf{W}_{[n]}$ is given by (where η is a small positive constant)

$$\mathbf{W}_{[n+1]} = \mathbf{W}_{[n]} + \Delta_{\mathbf{w}_{[n]}} = \mathbf{W}_{[n]} - \eta \nabla_g = \mathbf{W}_{[n]} - \eta \frac{\partial g(\mathbf{W}_{[n]})}{\partial \mathbf{W}_{[n]}}.$$

4. If $\mathbf{W}_{[n]} = \mathbf{W}_{[n+1]}$ (or $\mathbf{W}_{[n]} \approx \mathbf{W}_{[n+1]}$ when an approximation is sufficient), stop the procedure, else reiterate Steps 1 and 2.

3.11.2 The Widrow-Hoff Rule Is Gradient Descent

For an autoassociator, the function to minimize is the error function defined as the sum of squares of the differences between the expected values $\mathbf{x}_k$ and the responses of the network $\widehat{\mathbf{x}}_k$. Specifically, the error function for the kth response is given by

$$\mathcal{J}_k = \tfrac{1}{2}(\mathbf{x}_k - \widehat{\mathbf{x}}_k)^T(\mathbf{x}_k - \widehat{\mathbf{x}}_k) = \tfrac{1}{2}(\mathbf{x}_k^T\mathbf{x}_k + \widehat{\mathbf{x}}_k^T\widehat{\mathbf{x}}_k - 2\mathbf{x}_k^T\widehat{\mathbf{x}}_k) \quad (3.23)$$

(the multiplicative factor of $\tfrac{1}{2}$ is here only for convenience).

The gradient of $\mathcal{J}_k$ relative to $\mathbf{W}$ is computed using the chain rule adapted to matrices (Abdi, 1994a, p. 202$f\!f.$; Magnus & Neudecker, 1988): $\nabla_\mathbf{W}\mathcal{J}_k = \dfrac{\partial \mathcal{J}_k}{\partial \mathbf{W}} = \dfrac{\partial \mathcal{J}_k}{\partial \widehat{\mathbf{x}}_k}\dfrac{\partial \widehat{\mathbf{x}}_k}{\partial \mathbf{W}}$ with $\dfrac{\partial \mathcal{J}_k}{\partial \widehat{\mathbf{x}}_k} = -(\mathbf{x}_k - \widehat{\mathbf{x}}_k)$, and $\dfrac{\partial \widehat{\mathbf{x}}_k}{\partial \mathbf{W}} = \dfrac{\partial \mathbf{W}^T\mathbf{x}_k}{\partial \mathbf{W}} = 2\mathbf{x}_k^T$. Therefore, the correction for $\mathbf{W}$ at iteration n is proportional to $-\nabla_\mathbf{W}\mathcal{J}_k = (\mathbf{x}_k - \widehat{\mathbf{x}}_k)\mathbf{x}_k^T$, which, using η as a proportionality constant, gives the single stimulus mode Widrow-Hoff learning rule of Eq. 3.15 on page 38.

4. LINEAR HETEROASSOCIATIVE MEMORIES

4.1 Overview

Heteroassociative memories are composed of two layers of linear units—an input layer and an output layer—connected by a set of modifiable connections. They differ from autoassociative memories in that an input pattern is associated to an output pattern instead of being associated to itself. The goal of a heteroassociative memory is to learn mappings between input-output pairs such that the memory produces the appropriate output in response to a given input pattern.

Heteroassociative memories are generally used to solve pattern identification and categorization problems. They differ from the perceptron presented in Chapter 2 in that their basic units are linear and their input and output continuous. From a statistical point of view the inner working of a heteroassociative memory is equivalent to the technique of multiple linear regression and can be analyzed using the mathematical tools detailed in the chapter on autoassociative memories (i.e., least squares estimation and eigen- or singular value decomposition). From a cognitivist point of view, their interest comes

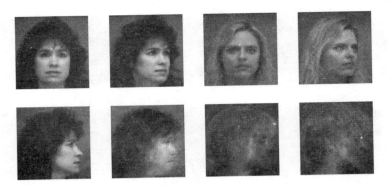

Figure 4.1: Responses of a heteroassociative memory trained to associate frontal and profile views of 20 female faces. The top row represents the images presented as memory keys and the bottom row the images reconstructed by the memory. The association between the frontal view and the profile view at the extreme left was learned. The other associations were not learned.

from the fact that they provide a way of simulating the associative properties of human memories.

As an application example, Fig. 4.1 illustrates the performance of a heteroassociative memory trained to associate frontal and profile views of 20 female faces.[1] After learning completion, the ability of the memory to produce profile views of learned faces in response to a frontal or a 3/4 view of the faces was evaluated along with the memory's ability to generalize to new faces. For a learned face (left panels), the memory response to the input of a frontal view is an exact profile view, but the response to a 3/4 view is only an approximate profile view. For faces not learned (right panels), the quality of the profile approximation decreases.

4.2 Architecture of a Heteroassociative Memory

The building blocks of linear heteroassociative memories are the basic linear units described in Chapter 3 (see illustration Fig. 3.2 on page 22). Specifically, a linear heteroassociative memory is a network composed of I input units connected to J output units. Each output unit receives inputs from all the input units, sums them, and transforms the sum into a response via a linear transfer function. The set

---

[1]The face images were represented as vectors of pixel intensities obtained by concatenation of the columns of digitized photographic images.

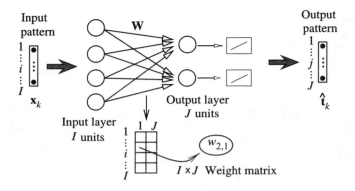

Figure 4.2: Architecture of a heteroassociative memory.

of connections between input and output units is represented by an $I \times J$ matrix $\mathbf{W}$:

$$\mathbf{W} = \begin{bmatrix} w_{1,1} & w_{1,2} & \cdots & w_{1,J} \\ w_{2,1} & w_{2,2} & \cdots & w_{2,J} \\ \vdots & \vdots & \ddots & \vdots \\ w_{I,1} & w_{I,2} & \cdots & w_{I,J} \end{bmatrix} . \tag{4.1}$$

In this matrix, a given element $w_{i,j}$ represents the strength of the connection between the ith input unit and the jth output unit.

Each of the K input patterns is represented by an I-dimensional vector denoted $\mathbf{x}_k$. Each of the K corresponding output patterns is represented by a J-dimensional vector denoted $\mathbf{t}_k$. The set of K input patterns is represented by an $I \times K$ matrix denoted $\mathbf{X}$ in which the kth column corresponds to the kth input vector $\mathbf{x}_k$. Likewise, the set of K output patterns is represented by a $J \times K$ matrix denoted $\mathbf{T}$ in which the kth column corresponds to the kth output vector $\mathbf{t}_k$. Learning of the mapping between input-output pairs is done by modifying the strength of the connections between input and output units. These modifications can be implemented using the two learning rules described in Chapter 3 (i.e., Hebbian and Widrow-Hoff).

4.3 The Hebbian Learning Rule

Remember that Hebb's learning rule states that the strength of the synapse between two neurons is a function of the temporal correlation between the two neurons (e.g., it increases whenever they fire simultaneously). In a heteroassociative memory:

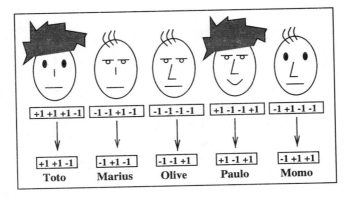

Figure 4.3: Face-name pairs to be stored in a heteroassociative memory.

> *The Hebbian learning rule sets the change of the connection weights to be proportional to the product of the input and the expected output.*

Formally, a set of K input-output pairs is stored in a heteroassociative memory by multiplying each input pattern vector by the corresponding output pattern vector and summing the resulting outer-product matrices. Specifically, the connection weight matrix is obtained with Hebbian learning as

$$\mathbf{W} = \gamma \sum_{k=1}^{K} \mathbf{x}_k \mathbf{t}_k^T , \qquad (4.2)$$

where γ represents the proportionality constant. Note that, in this case, the Hebbian learning rule could be considered as a supervised type of learning because the correct output is used during learning. A completely unsupervised version of this rule also exists in which the actual output vector is associated with the input vector instead of the expected output. This version of the rule is, however, seldom used (see Hagan, Demuth, & Beale, 1996, for some examples).

4.3.1 Numerical Example: Face and Name Association

Imagine that you want to train a linear heteroassociative memory to identify a sample of the schematic faces described in Chapter 3. Recall that these faces are made of four features (hair, eyes, nose, and mouth), each taking either the value $+1$ or -1, and can be represented as 4-dimensional binary vectors. For example, the five faces displayed in Fig. 4.3 can be represented by the following five vectors:

$$\mathbf{x}_1 = \begin{bmatrix} +1 \\ +1 \\ +1 \\ -1 \end{bmatrix}, \; \mathbf{x}_2 = \begin{bmatrix} -1 \\ -1 \\ +1 \\ -1 \end{bmatrix}, \; \mathbf{x}_3 = \begin{bmatrix} -1 \\ -1 \\ -1 \\ -1 \end{bmatrix}, \; \mathbf{x}_4 = \begin{bmatrix} +1 \\ -1 \\ -1 \\ +1 \end{bmatrix}, \; \mathbf{x}_5 = \begin{bmatrix} -1 \\ +1 \\ -1 \\ -1 \end{bmatrix}$$

or, equivalently, by a 4×5 matrix $\mathbf{X}$:

$$\mathbf{X} = \begin{bmatrix} 1 & -1 & -1 & 1 & -1 \\ 1 & -1 & -1 & -1 & 1 \\ 1 & 1 & -1 & -1 & -1 \\ -1 & -1 & -1 & 1 & -1 \end{bmatrix},$$

in which the first column represents the first face ($\mathbf{x}_1$), the second column the second face ($\mathbf{x}_2$), and so on.

The five names to be associated to the faces are represented by 3-dimensional arbitrary binary vectors denoted $\mathbf{t}_k$ corresponding to the names of "Toto," "Marius," "Olive," "Paulo," and "Momo":

$$\mathbf{t}_1 = \begin{bmatrix} +1 \\ +1 \\ -1 \end{bmatrix}, \mathbf{t}_2 = \begin{bmatrix} -1 \\ +1 \\ -1 \end{bmatrix}, \mathbf{t}_3 = \begin{bmatrix} -1 \\ -1 \\ +1 \end{bmatrix}, \mathbf{t}_4 = \begin{bmatrix} +1 \\ -1 \\ +1 \end{bmatrix}, \text{ and } \mathbf{t}_5 = \begin{bmatrix} -1 \\ +1 \\ +1 \end{bmatrix}.$$

The set of five names can also be stored in a 3×5 matrix, denoted $\mathbf{T}$:

$$\mathbf{T} = \begin{bmatrix} 1 & -1 & -1 & 1 & -1 \\ 1 & 1 & -1 & -1 & 1 \\ -1 & -1 & 1 & 1 & 1 \end{bmatrix}.$$

The first column in $\mathbf{T}$ represents the name of the first face (Toto), the second column the name of the second face (Marius), and so on.

Identifying a face, in this context, means associating the face with its name. Training the memory to identify the faces thus amounts to having it learn each of the following pairs of input-output patterns:

$$\mathbf{x}_1 = \begin{bmatrix} +1 \\ +1 \\ +1 \\ -1 \end{bmatrix} \longmapsto \mathbf{t}_1 = \begin{bmatrix} +1 \\ +1 \\ -1 \end{bmatrix}, \; \mathbf{x}_2 \begin{bmatrix} -1 \\ -1 \\ +1 \\ -1 \end{bmatrix} \longmapsto \mathbf{t}_2 = \begin{bmatrix} -1 \\ +1 \\ -1 \end{bmatrix}$$

$$\mathbf{x}_3 = \begin{bmatrix} -1 \\ -1 \\ -1 \\ -1 \end{bmatrix} \longmapsto \mathbf{t}_3 = \begin{bmatrix} -1 \\ -1 \\ +1 \end{bmatrix}, \; \mathbf{x}_4 \begin{bmatrix} +1 \\ -1 \\ -1 \\ +1 \end{bmatrix} \longmapsto \mathbf{t}_4 = \begin{bmatrix} +1 \\ -1 \\ +1 \end{bmatrix}$$

$$\mathbf{x}_5 = \begin{bmatrix} -1 \\ +1 \\ -1 \\ -1 \end{bmatrix} \longmapsto \mathbf{t}_5 = \begin{bmatrix} -1 \\ +1 \\ +1 \end{bmatrix}.$$

The memory then is said to have learned to identify the faces if it gives back the correct name when prompted with a face.

For example, if the memory is prompted with the vector $\mathbf{x}_3 = [-1 \quad -1 \quad -1 \quad -1]^T$ representing Face 3 in Fig. 4.3, it should give back the vector $\mathbf{t}_3 = [-1 \quad -1 \quad +1]^T$ representing the name "Olive."

4.3.1.1 Steps in Building the Weight Matrix

To store a face-name association in the heteroassociative memory, each element of the face vector is used as input to a cell of the memory input layer and each input cell is connected to every cell of the output layer. The values of the connection strengths between input and output cells are stored in the 4×3 matrix $\mathbf{W}$. As for the autoassociative memory, we assume that the connection strengths are initialized with zero values. The initial weight matrix, denoted $\mathbf{W}_{[0]}$, is thus equal to

$$\mathbf{W}_{[0]} = \begin{bmatrix} 0 & 0 & 0 \\ 0 & 0 & 0 \\ 0 & 0 & 0 \\ 0 & 0 & 0 \end{bmatrix}.$$

Step 1. The first face-name pair is stored in the memory by modifying the values of the connection weights following Eq. 4.2 with (for simplicity) a proportionality constant $\gamma = 1$:

$$\mathbf{W}_{[1]} = \mathbf{W}_{[0]} + \mathbf{x}_1 \mathbf{t}_1^T$$

$$= \begin{bmatrix} 0 & 0 & 0 \\ 0 & 0 & 0 \\ 0 & 0 & 0 \\ 0 & 0 & 0 \end{bmatrix} + \begin{bmatrix} +1 \\ +1 \\ +1 \\ -1 \end{bmatrix} [+1 \quad +1 \quad -1] = \begin{bmatrix} 1 & 1 & -1 \\ 1 & 1 & -1 \\ 1 & 1 & -1 \\ -1 & -1 & 1 \end{bmatrix}.$$

Observation of $\mathbf{W}_{[1]}$ shows that each time an input and an output unit are both positive or both negative, the weight between the two units increases by $+1$ and each time an input and an output unit have opposite values, the weight between the two units decreases by 1.

Step 2. The second face-name pair is stored in the memory:

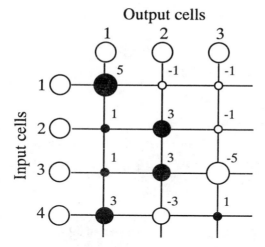

Figure 4.4: Connectivity pattern of a heteroassociative memory trained to identify the set of faces in Fig 4.3. The magnitude of the synaptic weight is represented by the area of the circles and their sign by the color of the circles (black circles for positive values, white circles for negative values).

$$\mathbf{W}_{[2]} = \mathbf{W}_{[1]} + \mathbf{x}_2 \mathbf{t}_2^T$$

$$= \begin{bmatrix} 1 & 1 & -1 \\ 1 & 1 & -1 \\ 1 & 1 & -1 \\ -1 & -1 & 1 \end{bmatrix} + \begin{bmatrix} -1 \\ -1 \\ +1 \\ -1 \end{bmatrix} \begin{bmatrix} -1 & +1 & -1 \end{bmatrix} = \begin{bmatrix} 2 & 0 & 0 \\ 2 & 0 & 0 \\ 0 & 2 & -2 \\ 0 & -2 & 2 \end{bmatrix}$$

and so on up to the fifth face-name pair.

Step 5. The last face-name pair is stored in the memory:

$$\mathbf{W}_{[5]} = \mathbf{W}_{[4]} + \mathbf{x}_5 \mathbf{t}_5^T$$

$$= \begin{bmatrix} 4 & 0 & 0 \\ 2 & 2 & -2 \\ 0 & 4 & -4 \\ 2 & -2 & 2 \end{bmatrix} + \begin{bmatrix} -1 \\ +1 \\ -1 \\ -1 \end{bmatrix} \begin{bmatrix} -1 & +1 & +1 \end{bmatrix} = \begin{bmatrix} 5 & -1 & -1 \\ 1 & 3 & -1 \\ 1 & 3 & -5 \\ 3 & -3 & 1 \end{bmatrix}$$

and we now have the complete connection matrix. Note that this matrix illustrated in Fig. 4.4 could have been obtained more directly using matrix multiplication as $\mathbf{W} = \mathbf{X}\mathbf{T}^T$.

4.3.2 Performance Evaluation

The ability of the memory to produce the output pattern corresponding to a given input pattern is tested by premultiplying the input vector, $\mathbf{x}_k$, by the transpose of the weight matrix, $\mathbf{W}^T$, and comparing the memory response, denoted $\widehat{\mathbf{t}}_k$, with the expected output. The response, $\widehat{\mathbf{t}}_k$, is computed as $\widehat{\mathbf{t}}_k = \mathbf{W}^T \mathbf{x}_k$. The quality of the response is evaluated by computing the cosine: $\cos\left(\widehat{\mathbf{t}}_k, \mathbf{t}_k\right)$.

4.3.2.1 Back to the Numerical Example

Suppose you want to test if the memory can produce the name "Toto" when Face 1 is presented as a memory key. First, the transpose of the weight matrix is (post)multiplied by the vector representing Face 1.

$$\widehat{\mathbf{t}}_1 = \mathbf{W}^T \mathbf{x}_1 = \begin{bmatrix} 5 & 1 & 1 & 3 \\ -1 & 3 & 3 & -3 \\ -1 & -1 & -5 & 1 \end{bmatrix} \begin{bmatrix} +1 \\ +1 \\ +1 \\ -1 \end{bmatrix} = \begin{bmatrix} +4 \\ +8 \\ -8 \end{bmatrix}.$$

The response $\widehat{\mathbf{t}}_1 = [+4 \ \ +8 \ \ -8]^T$ is then compared to the expected output (coding the name "Toto") $\mathbf{t}_1 = [+1 \ \ +1 \ \ -1]^T$. This shows that, although the patterns of $+$ and $-$ are similar, the two vectors are different and hence the name associated to the first face is somewhat distorted. This is confirmed by computing the cosine:

$$\cos\left(\widehat{\mathbf{t}}_1, \mathbf{t}_1\right) = \frac{\widehat{\mathbf{t}}_1^T \mathbf{t}_1}{\|\widehat{\mathbf{t}}_1\| \, \|\mathbf{t}_1\|} = \frac{16}{\sqrt{96}\sqrt{3}} = \frac{16}{16.97} = .9428.$$

4.3.2.2 Matrix Notation

Note that, once again, recall of the full set of learned patterns can be achieved in a single step using matrix multiplication $\widehat{\mathbf{T}} = \mathbf{W}^T \mathbf{X}$. For our example, we obtain:

$$\widehat{\mathbf{T}} = \mathbf{W}^T \mathbf{X} = \begin{bmatrix} 5 & 1 & 1 & 3 \\ -1 & 3 & 3 & -3 \\ -1 & -1 & -5 & 1 \end{bmatrix} \times \begin{bmatrix} 1 & -1 & -1 & 1 & -1 \\ 1 & -1 & -1 & -1 & 1 \\ 1 & 1 & -1 & -1 & -1 \\ -1 & -1 & -1 & 1 & -1 \end{bmatrix}$$

$$= \begin{bmatrix} 4 & -8 & -10 & 6 & -8 \\ 8 & 4 & -2 & -10 & 4 \\ -8 & -4 & 6 & 6 & 4 \end{bmatrix},$$

where the first column is the response of the memory to Face 1, the second column the response of the memory to Face 2, and so on.

4.3.3 Orthogonality and Crosstalk

Comparing the response matrix from the previous section to the vectors coding the face names shows that none of the names associated with the faces is perfectly recalled. This happens because when the input vectors are not orthogonal (see Section 3.6.3 on page 33), the memory adds some noise to the expected patterns. Precisely:

$$\hat{\mathbf{t}}_\ell = \mathbf{W}^T \mathbf{x}_\ell = \sum_k \mathbf{t}_k \mathbf{x}_k^T \mathbf{x}_\ell$$

$$= \sum_k (\mathbf{x}_k^T \mathbf{x}_\ell) \mathbf{t}_k = (\mathbf{x}_\ell^T \mathbf{x}_\ell) \mathbf{t}_\ell + \sum_{k \neq \ell} (\mathbf{x}_k^T \mathbf{x}_\ell) \mathbf{t}_k. \tag{4.3}$$

The term $\sum_{k \neq \ell} (\mathbf{x}_k^T \mathbf{x}_\ell) \mathbf{t}_k$ is the interference or crosstalk between the response corresponding to the input pattern and the responses corresponding to the other stored patterns. When all the input patterns are pairwise orthogonal, all the scalar products between pairs of different vectors are equal to zero and hence $\sum_{k \neq \ell} (\mathbf{x}_k^T \mathbf{x}_\ell) \mathbf{t}_k = 0$. In this case, the response of the memory to an input pattern is equal to the expected output amplified by the scalar product of the input vector and itself $(\mathbf{x}_\ell^T \mathbf{x}_\ell)$. If the input pattern is normalized such that $\mathbf{x}_\ell^T \mathbf{x}_\ell = 1$, the response of the memory is the expected output.

If the input patterns are not orthogonal, the response of the memory is equal to the expected output amplified by the scalar product of the input vector and itself $(\mathbf{x}_\ell^T \mathbf{x}_\ell)$, plus the crosstalk component: $\sum_{k \neq \ell} (\mathbf{x}_k^T \mathbf{x}_\ell) \mathbf{t}_k$. The magnitude of the crosstalk depends on the similarity or correlation between the input patterns: The larger the similarity between the input patterns, the larger the crosstalk.

4.4 The Widrow-Hoff Learning Rule

The performance of the memory can be improved by using an error correction learning rule instead of the simple Hebbian learning rule. In this section we show how to extend the Widrow-Hoff learning rule, presented in Chapters 2 and 3, to the more general case of heteroassociative memories. Remember that the Widrow-Hoff learning rule adjusts the weights of the connections between cells so as to minimize the error sum of squares between the responses of the memory and the expected responses. The values of the weights are iteratively corrected using, as an error term, the difference between the expected output and the answer of the memory. This algorithm can be used either in a *single stimulus learning* mode (i.e., the error is computed after each stimulus) or in a *batch* mode (i.e., the error is computed for the complete set of patterns). As for the autoassociative memory, the two modes of learning converge to the same solution. We present first the faster of these two modes, the batch mode. The weight matrix for a heteroassociative memory at iteration $n + 1$ is expressed as

$$\mathbf{W}^T_{[n+1]} = \mathbf{W}^T_{[n]} + \eta(\mathbf{T} - \mathbf{W}^T_{[n]}\mathbf{X})\mathbf{X}^T = \mathbf{W}^T_{[n]} + \eta(\mathbf{T} - \widehat{\mathbf{T}}_{[n]})\mathbf{X}^T$$

$$= \mathbf{W}^T_{[n]} + \eta\mathbf{E}\mathbf{X}^T = \mathbf{W}^T_{[n]} + \Delta\mathbf{w}_{[n]}, \tag{4.4}$$

where n represents the iteration number, η a small positive constant, $\mathbf{E}$ the error matrix, and $\Delta\mathbf{w}_{[n]}$ the matrix of corrections for $\mathbf{W}$ at the nth iteration. For the single stimulus mode, Eq. 4.4 becomes

$$\mathbf{W}^T_{[n+1]} = \mathbf{W}^T_{[n]} + \eta(\mathbf{t}_k - \mathbf{W}^T_{[n]}\mathbf{x}_k)\mathbf{x}^T_k = \mathbf{W}^T_{[n]} + \Delta\mathbf{w}_{[n]}, \tag{4.5}$$

where k is a random integer $(1 \leq k \leq K)$.

4.4.1 Back to Associating Faces and Names

As an illustration of Widrow-Hoff learning, we will train a memory to identify the first two faces presented in Fig. 4.3. These faces can be represented by the 4×2 matrix $\mathbf{X}$ and their respective names, "Toto" and "Marius," by the 3×2 matrix $\mathbf{T}$:

$$\mathbf{X} = \begin{bmatrix} 1 & -1 \\ 1 & -1 \\ 1 & 1 \\ -1 & -1 \end{bmatrix} \qquad \mathbf{T} = \begin{bmatrix} 1 & -1 \\ 1 & 1 \\ -1 & -1 \end{bmatrix}.$$

We start by initializing the weight matrix to zeros:

$$\mathbf{W}_{[0]} = \begin{bmatrix} 0 & 0 & 0 \\ 0 & 0 & 0 \\ 0 & 0 & 0 \\ 0 & 0 & 0 \end{bmatrix}$$

and setting the learning constant η to .3. We are now ready to start the iterations described in Eq. 4.4.

4.4.1.1 Iteration 1

Step 1: Identify the faces

$$\widehat{\mathbf{T}}_{[0]} = \mathbf{W}^T_{[0]}\mathbf{X} = \begin{bmatrix} 0 & 0 & 0 & 0 \\ 0 & 0 & 0 & 0 \\ 0 & 0 & 0 & 0 \end{bmatrix} \times \begin{bmatrix} 1 & -1 \\ 1 & -1 \\ 1 & 1 \\ -1 & -1 \end{bmatrix} = \begin{bmatrix} 0 & 0 \\ 0 & 0 \\ 0 & 0 \end{bmatrix}.$$

Step 2: Compute the error

$$\mathbf{E}_{[0]} = \mathbf{T} - \widehat{\mathbf{T}}_{[0]} = \begin{bmatrix} 1 & -1 \\ 1 & 1 \\ -1 & -1 \end{bmatrix} - \begin{bmatrix} 0 & 0 \\ 0 & 0 \\ 0 & 0 \end{bmatrix} = \begin{bmatrix} 1 & -1 \\ 1 & 1 \\ -1 & -1 \end{bmatrix}.$$

Step 3: Compute the matrix of corrections

$$\boldsymbol{\Delta}\mathbf{w}_{[0]} = .3 \times \mathbf{E}_{[0]}\mathbf{X}^T = .3 \begin{bmatrix} 1 & -1 \\ 1 & 1 \\ -1 & -1 \end{bmatrix} \begin{bmatrix} 1 & 1 & 1 & -1 \\ -1 & -1 & 1 & -1 \end{bmatrix}$$

$$= \begin{bmatrix} .6 & .6 & 0 & 0 \\ 0 & 0 & .6 & -.6 \\ 0 & 0 & -.6 & .6 \end{bmatrix}.$$

Step 4: Update the weight matrix

$$\mathbf{W}^T_{[1]} = \mathbf{W}^T_{[0]} + \boldsymbol{\Delta}\mathbf{w}_{[0]} = \begin{bmatrix} 0 & 0 & 0 & 0 \\ 0 & 0 & 0 & 0 \\ 0 & 0 & 0 & 0 \end{bmatrix} + \begin{bmatrix} .6 & .6 & 0 & 0 \\ 0 & 0 & .6 & -.6 \\ 0 & 0 & -.6 & .6 \end{bmatrix}$$

$$= \begin{bmatrix} .6 & .6 & 0 & 0 \\ 0 & 0 & .6 & -.6 \\ 0 & 0 & -.6 & .6 \end{bmatrix} \dots \text{ and so on up to}$$

4.4.1.2 Iteration 16

$$\widehat{\mathbf{T}}_{[15]} = \mathbf{W}^T_{[15]}\mathbf{X} = \begin{bmatrix} .5 & .5 & 0 & 0 \\ 0 & 0 & .5 & -.5 \\ 0 & 0 & -.5 & .5 \end{bmatrix} \times \begin{bmatrix} 1 & -1 \\ 1 & -1 \\ 1 & 1 \\ -1 & -1 \end{bmatrix} = \begin{bmatrix} 1 & -1 \\ 1 & 1 \\ -1 & -1 \end{bmatrix}$$

$$\mathbf{E}_{[15]} = \mathbf{T} - \widehat{\mathbf{T}}_{[15]} = \begin{bmatrix} 1 & -1 \\ 1 & 1 \\ -1 & -1 \end{bmatrix} - \begin{bmatrix} 1 & -1 \\ 1 & 1 \\ -1 & -1 \end{bmatrix} = \begin{bmatrix} 0 & 0 \\ 0 & 0 \\ 0 & 0 \end{bmatrix}$$

$$\boldsymbol{\Delta}\mathbf{w}_{[15]} = .3 \times \mathbf{E}_{[15]}\mathbf{X}^T = .3 \begin{bmatrix} 0 & 0 \\ 0 & 0 \\ 0 & 0 \end{bmatrix} \begin{bmatrix} 1 & 1 & 1 & -1 \\ -1 & -1 & 1 & -1 \end{bmatrix} = \begin{bmatrix} 0 & 0 & 0 & 0 \\ 0 & 0 & 0 & 0 \\ 0 & 0 & 0 & 0 \end{bmatrix}.$$

Et voilà! The faces are perfectly identified after 16 iterations.

4.4.2 Widrow-Hoff and Eigendecomposition

As for the autoassociative memory, the Widrow-Hoff learning rule can be expressed from the singular value decomposition (SVD) of $\mathbf{X}$. Precisely, the batch mode version (*cf.* Eq. 4.4 on page 55) can be implemented as

$$\mathbf{W}_{[n]}^T = \mathbf{TV\Delta}^{-1}\mathbf{\Phi}_{[n]}\mathbf{U}^T \text{ with } \mathbf{\Phi}_{[n]} = \mathbf{I} - (\mathbf{I} - \eta\mathbf{\Lambda})^n, \qquad (4.6)$$

where n is the iteration number, $\mathbf{U}$ is the matrix of eigenvectors of $\mathbf{XX}^T$, $\mathbf{V}$ is the matrix of eigenvectors of $\mathbf{X}^T\mathbf{X}$, and $\mathbf{\Delta}$ is the diagonal matrix of singular values of $\mathbf{X}$ (for a notation refresher, see also Section 3.10 pages 41*ff.*). For stimulus mode learning, Eq. 4.6 gives the state of the matrix after the nth learning epoch.

When η is properly chosen,[2] $\mathbf{\Phi}_{[n]}$ converges to $\mathbf{I}$ and $\mathbf{W}$ becomes

$$\mathbf{W}_{[\infty]}^T = \mathbf{TV\Delta}^{-1}\mathbf{U}^T. \qquad (4.7)$$

For the previous example, the SVD of $\mathbf{X}$ gives

$$\mathbf{X} = \mathbf{U\Delta V}^T = \begin{bmatrix} 1 & -1 \\ 1 & -1 \\ 1 & 1 \\ -1 & -1 \end{bmatrix} = \begin{bmatrix} -.5 & .5 \\ -.5 & .5 \\ .5 & .5 \\ -.5 & -.5 \end{bmatrix} \times \begin{bmatrix} 2 & 0 \\ 0 & 2 \end{bmatrix} \times \begin{bmatrix} 0 & 1 \\ 1 & 0 \end{bmatrix}.$$

With a learning constant $\eta = .3$, the weight matrix at iteration 1 is obtained as $\mathbf{W}_{[1]}^T = \mathbf{TV\Delta}^{-1}\mathbf{\Phi}_{[1]}\mathbf{U}^T$, with

$$\mathbf{\Phi}_{[1]} = \mathbf{I} - (\mathbf{I} - \eta\mathbf{\Lambda})^1 = \begin{bmatrix} 1 & 0 \\ 0 & 1 \end{bmatrix} - \left\{ \begin{bmatrix} 1 & 0 \\ 0 & 1 \end{bmatrix} - .3 \times \begin{bmatrix} 4 & 0 \\ 0 & 4 \end{bmatrix} \right\}^1$$

$$= \begin{bmatrix} 1.2 & 0 \\ 0 & 1.2 \end{bmatrix}, \quad \text{which gives}$$

$$\mathbf{W}_{[1]}^T = \begin{bmatrix} 1 & -1 \\ 1 & 1 \\ -1 & -1 \end{bmatrix} \times \begin{bmatrix} 0 & 1 \\ 1 & 0 \end{bmatrix} \times \begin{bmatrix} \frac{1}{2} & 0 \\ 0 & \frac{1}{2} \end{bmatrix} \times \begin{bmatrix} 1.2 & 0 \\ 0 & 1.2 \end{bmatrix}$$

$$\times \begin{bmatrix} -.5 & -.5 & .5 & -.5 \\ .5 & .5 & .5 & -.5 \end{bmatrix} = \begin{bmatrix} .6 & .6 & 0 & 0 \\ 0 & 0 & .6 & -.6 \\ 0 & 0 & -.6 & .6 \end{bmatrix}$$

---

[2]Precisely, η should satisfy the following condition (*cf.* Eq. 3.22 on page 43 for autoassociative memories): $0 < \eta < 2\delta_{max}^{-2}$, where δ_{max} is the largest singular value of $\mathbf{X}$ (see Abdi, 1994a, pp. 54–59 for a proof).

and so on up to

$$\mathbf{W}^T_{[\infty]} = \mathbf{TV\Delta}^{-1}\mathbf{U}^T$$

$$= \begin{bmatrix} 1 & -1 \\ 1 & 1 \\ -1 & -1 \end{bmatrix} \times \begin{bmatrix} 0 & 1 \\ 1 & 0 \end{bmatrix} \times \begin{bmatrix} \frac{1}{2} & 0 \\ 0 & \frac{1}{2} \end{bmatrix} \times \begin{bmatrix} -.5 & -.5 & .5 & -.5 \\ .5 & .5 & .5 & -.5 \end{bmatrix}$$

$$= \begin{bmatrix} .5 & .5 & 0 & 0 \\ 0 & 0 & .5 & -.5 \\ 0 & 0 & -.5 & .5 \end{bmatrix}.$$

These are the same values given for $\mathbf{W}_{[15]}$ in Section 4.4.1.2 (page 56).

4.5 Widrow-Hoff, Pseudo-Inverse, and Linear Regression

4.5.1 Overview

Remember that the goal of a heteroassociator is to learn the mapping between pairs of input-output patterns so that the correct output is produced when a given pattern is presented as a memory key. Formally, this goal is achieved by finding the connection weights between the input and output units so that

$$\mathbf{T} = \mathbf{W}^T\mathbf{X}. \tag{4.8}$$

In the previous sections we have seen that Hebbian learning is one way of finding the values of $\mathbf{W}$. However, when the input patterns are not orthogonal, this learning mechanism suffers from interference or crosstalk and produces some errors. As we showed, this problem can be overcome by using the Widrow-Hoff error correction learning rule. In this section we show that an equivalent way of finding the values of $\mathbf{W}$ is to solve Eq. 4.8. If the matrix $\mathbf{X}$ has an inverse,[3] the solution is simply

$$\mathbf{W}^T = \mathbf{TX}^{-1}. \tag{4.9}$$

However, in most applications, the matrix of stimuli $\mathbf{X}$ does not have an inverse. For example, the 4×2 face matrix $\mathbf{X}$ presented in the previous example, is obviously not a square matrix and hence is not invertible. In that case, we want to find the values of $\mathbf{W}$ such that the response produced by the memory will be as similar as possible to the expected response. More formally, we want to find $\mathbf{W}$ such that

---

[3]Remember that only full rank square matrices have an inverse.

the squared distance between the actual output ($\mathbf{T}$) and the desired output ($\widehat{\mathbf{T}} = \mathbf{W}^T\mathbf{X}$) is minimum. Specifically, we want to obtain a matrix $\mathbf{W}$ such that

$$\mathcal{J} = \tfrac{1}{2} \text{trace}\left\{ (\mathbf{T} - \mathbf{W}^T\mathbf{X})^T (\mathbf{T} - \mathbf{W}^T\mathbf{X}) \right\} \quad (4.10)$$

is minimum over all possible $I \times J$ real matrices. The weight matrix that satisfies this constraint is given by the *pseudo-inverse rule*:

$$\mathbf{W}^T = \mathbf{T}\mathbf{X}^+, \quad (4.11)$$

where $\mathbf{X}^+$ is the Moore-Penrose pseudo-inverse of $\mathbf{X}$ described in the following section (see, e.g., Abdi, 1994a, for a proof).

4.5.2 Pseudo-Inverse and Singular Value Decomposition

The Moore-Penrose or pseudo-inverse was discovered independently by Moore in the 1920s and later by Penrose (Searle, 1982). It is the optimal least squares solution of any system of linear equations such as the one described in Eq. 4.8. Formally, the pseudo-inverse of matrix $\mathbf{X}$, denoted $\mathbf{X}^+$, is the unique matrix that satisfies these 4 conditions:

$$\begin{aligned} \mathbf{X}\mathbf{X}^+\mathbf{X} &= \mathbf{X} & i \\ \mathbf{X}^+\mathbf{X}\mathbf{X}^+ &= \mathbf{X}^+ & ii \\ \mathbf{X}^+\mathbf{X} &= (\mathbf{X}^+\mathbf{X})^T & iii \\ \mathbf{X}\mathbf{X}^+ &= (\mathbf{X}\mathbf{X}^+)^T & iv \,. \end{aligned} \quad (4.12)$$

When the matrix $\mathbf{X}$ is invertible, its pseudo-inverse $\mathbf{X}^+$ is equal to its inverse $\mathbf{X}^{-1}$. The pseudo-inverse of a matrix can be computed via the singular value decomposition of the matrix (see Chapter 3, pages 41*ff*.). Specifically, if $\mathbf{X} = \mathbf{U}\boldsymbol{\Delta}\mathbf{V}^T$, then the pseudo-inverse of $\mathbf{X}$ can be obtained by pseudo-inverting the three factors $\mathbf{U}$, $\boldsymbol{\Delta}$, and $\mathbf{V}^T$ of $\mathbf{X}$ separately and multiplying them in the reverse order: $\mathbf{X}^+ = (\mathbf{V}^T)^+\boldsymbol{\Delta}^+\mathbf{U}^+$. Because the inverse of an orthogonal matrix is equal to its transpose and $\boldsymbol{\Delta}$ is a diagonal matrix, the previous equation reduces to

$$\mathbf{X}^+ = \mathbf{V}\boldsymbol{\Delta}^{-1}\mathbf{U}^T \,. \quad (4.13)$$

For our previous example, we obtain

$$\mathbf{X}^+ = \begin{bmatrix} 0 & 1 \\ 1 & 0 \end{bmatrix} \times \begin{bmatrix} .5 & 0 \\ 0 & .5 \end{bmatrix} \times \begin{bmatrix} -.5 & -.5 & .5 & -.5 \\ .5 & .5 & .5 & -.5 \end{bmatrix}$$

$$= \begin{bmatrix} .25 & .25 & .25 & -.25 \\ -.25 & -.25 & .25 & -.25 \end{bmatrix} \,.$$

4.5.3 Back to the Weight Matrix and the Pseudo-Inverse

Comparing Eq. 4.7 to Eq. 4.13, we can see that, after convergence, the Widrow-Hoff learning rule gives for the system of linear equations $\mathbf{T} = \mathbf{W}^T\mathbf{X}$, the following (least squares) solution:

$$\mathbf{W}^T_{[\infty]} = \mathbf{T}\mathbf{V}\mathbf{\Delta}^{-1}\mathbf{U}^T = \mathbf{T}\mathbf{X}^+ . \tag{4.14}$$

As an illustration, let us compute the weight matrix of the previous example, using the pseudo-inverse of $\mathbf{X}$. Since we have already computed $\mathbf{X}^+$ in the previous section, it suffices to premultiply it by $\mathbf{T}$:

$$\mathbf{W}^T = \begin{bmatrix} 1 & -1 \\ 1 & 1 \\ -1 & -1 \end{bmatrix} \times \begin{bmatrix} .25 & .25 & .25 & -.25 \\ -.25 & -.25 & .25 & -.25 \end{bmatrix} = \begin{bmatrix} .5 & .5 & 0 & 0 \\ 0 & 0 & .5 & -.5 \\ 0 & 0 & -.5 & .5 \end{bmatrix}.$$

This gives back the value obtained using Widrow-Hoff learning.

4.6 The Widrow-Hoff Learning Rule and Gradient Descent

For a linear heteroassociator, the function to minimize is the error function defined as the sum of squares of the differences between the expected values $\mathbf{t}_k$ and the responses of the network $\widehat{\mathbf{t}}_k$. Specifically, the error function for response k is given by

$$\mathcal{J}_k = \tfrac{1}{2}(\mathbf{t}_k - \widehat{\mathbf{t}}_k)^T(\mathbf{t}_k - \widehat{\mathbf{t}}_k) = \tfrac{1}{2}(\mathbf{t}_k^T\mathbf{t}_k + \widehat{\mathbf{t}}_k^T\widehat{\mathbf{t}}_k - 2\mathbf{t}_k^T\widehat{\mathbf{t}}_k) \tag{4.15}$$

The gradient of $\mathcal{J}_k$ relative to $\mathbf{W}$ is computed using the chain rule adapted to matrices: $\nabla_{\mathbf{W}}\mathcal{J}_k = \dfrac{\partial \mathcal{J}_k}{\partial \mathbf{W}} = \dfrac{\partial \mathcal{J}_k}{\partial \widehat{\mathbf{t}}_k}\dfrac{\partial \widehat{\mathbf{t}}_k}{\partial \mathbf{W}}$ with $\dfrac{\partial \mathcal{J}_k}{\partial \widehat{\mathbf{t}}_k} = -(\mathbf{t}_k - \widehat{\mathbf{t}}_k)$, and $\dfrac{\partial \widehat{\mathbf{t}}_k}{\partial \mathbf{W}} = \dfrac{\partial \mathbf{W}^T\mathbf{x}_k}{\partial \mathbf{W}} = 2\mathbf{x}_k^T$. Therefore, the correction for $\mathbf{W}$ at iteration n is proportional to $-\nabla_{\mathbf{W}}\mathcal{J}_k = (\mathbf{t}_k - \widehat{\mathbf{t}}_k)\mathbf{x}_k^T$, which, using η as a proportionality constant, gives the single stimulus mode Widrow-Hoff learning rule of Eq. 4.5 on page 55.

4.7 Discriminant Analysis and Perceptron Revisited

Remember that the perceptron is akin to discriminant analysis but not identical (see page 20). A linear heteroassociative memory is, in some cases, equivalent to discriminant analysis. Specifically, Eq. 4.15 indicates that a linear heteroassociative memory with binary target values (i.e., learning two classes) is minimizing the same criterion as discriminant analysis. In fact, if the first class has n_1 elements and the second class n_2 elements, then target values of $-\dfrac{1}{n_1}$ for the first class and $\dfrac{1}{n_2}$ for the second class, cause the memory to use gradient descent to find a minimum of the linear discriminant function of Eq. 2.11 on page 20.

4.8 Radial Basis Function Networks

One of the limitations of linear heteroassociators is, indeed, their very linearity. This limitation can be overcome by adding a nonlinear component to the model. This can be done using several strategies. One strategy, which we present in the next chapter, consists of using a nonlinear transfer function to compute the response of a cell in conjunction with an error backpropagation learning algorithm. Another strategy, which we describe in this section, is to compute a nonlinear transformation of the input vectors via a radial basis function (RBF) network. RBFs are a recent addition to the neural-modeler's toolbox (Haykin, 1998). The architecture of a typical radial basis function network is shown in Fig. 4.5 on the following page.

RBF networks are used for approximating a nonlinear function as well as for finding interpolating values of a function defined only on a finite subset of real numbers. This nonlinear mapping is implemented from the input pattern space to the output pattern space as a two-step process. The first step is a simple nonlinear mapping from the input layer to the hidden layer. The second step implements a linear transformation from the hidden layer to the output layer. Learning occurs only at the level of the synapses between the hidden layer and the output layer. Because these connections are linear, learning is very fast. In brief, the main idea of RBF networks is as follows:

> *Replace the stimulus vectors using a nonlinear transformation such that each stimulus is represented by a vector coding its similarity to several arbitrary points called prototypes or centers, and then use a standard linear heteroassociator.*

4.8.1 Mathematical Foundations

The problem is to approximate an arbitrary function f from $\mathbb{R}^I$ to $\mathbb{R}^J$ (i.e., f associates a $J \times 1$ dimensional vector $\mathbf{t}_k$ in response to an

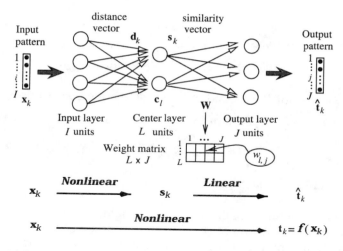

Figure 4.5: The architecture of a typical radial basis function network. The hidden layer computes the distance from the input to each of the centers (each center corresponds to a cell of the hidden layer). The cells of the hidden layer transform their activation (i.e., the distance from the input) into a response using a nonlinear transformation (typically a Gaussian function). The cells of the output layer behave like a standard linear heteroassociator.

$I \times 1$ dimensional vector $\mathbf{x}_k$) defined on K observations such that

$$\mathbf{t}_k = f(\mathbf{x}_k) \qquad \text{for } k = \{1, \ldots, K\} . \tag{4.16}$$

The general idea is to approximate f by a weighted sum of (in general nonlinear) functions ϕ (named the *basis* functions) such that the function in Eq. 4.16 is approximated by

$$\widehat{\mathbf{t}}_k \approx \sum_\ell v_\ell \phi(\mathbf{x}_k) , \tag{4.17}$$

with v_ℓ being a real number and $\phi(\mathbf{x}_k)$ a $J \times 1$ function vector (i.e., it gives back a $J \times 1$ vector in response to the $I \times 1$ vector $\mathbf{x}_k$). Some well-known methods using this approach are the discrete Fourier transform and the discrete wavelet transform.

This technique is called a *radial* basis function approximation if several "centers" are chosen (either arbitrarily or in some specific ways) and the *distance* from the vectors $\mathbf{x}_k$ to these centers is used in Eq. 4.17 instead of the $\mathbf{x}_k$ values. A center may be any I-dimensional vector (which guarantees that the distance between the center and each $\mathbf{x}_k$ is always defined).

Formally, if L centers $\mathbf{c}_\ell$ are chosen, Eq. 4.17 on the preceding page is approximated as

$$\widehat{\mathbf{t}}_k \approx \sum_\ell v_\ell \phi(\|\mathbf{x}_k - \mathbf{c}_\ell\|) = \sum_\ell v_\ell \phi(d_{\mathbf{c}_\ell, \mathbf{x}_k}) , \qquad (4.18)$$

with $d_{\mathbf{c}_\ell, \mathbf{x}_k}$ being the distance between vector $\mathbf{x}_k$ and center $\mathbf{c}_\ell$ and $\phi(d)$ a $J \times 1$ function vector. In general the Euclidean distance is used [$d^2_{\mathbf{c}_\ell, \mathbf{x}_k} = (\mathbf{c}_\ell - \mathbf{x}_k)^T (\mathbf{c}_\ell - \mathbf{x}_k)$], but other distances can be used.

When the set of centers (the $\mathbf{c}_\ell$'s) is the same set as the input set (i.e., the $\mathbf{x}_k$'s), the radial basis function network is used for finding an *interpolation* function valid for new values of $\mathbf{x}_{k'}$ and fitting f perfectly for the K observations $\mathbf{x}_k$. When the set of centers differs from the input set (i.e., the $\mathbf{x}_k$), it contains, in general, less centers than stimuli (i.e., $L < K$). The problem, then, can be seen as a problem of *approximating* the function f by a set of simpler functions ϕ. In both cases, the objective is close to some rather well-known techniques in numerical analysis (e.g., spline interpolations) with the difference that a distance to the centers is used in the process rather than the raw data.

4.8.2 Neural Network Implementation

In a neural network framework, this technique can be interpreted as first implementing a two-step transformation on the stimuli and then applying a standard heteroassociator (see Fig. 4.5 on the facing page). The first transformation step creates, for each $I \times 1$ stimulus vector $\mathbf{x}_k$, an $L \times 1$ distance vector $\mathbf{d}_k$ (each element of $\mathbf{d}_k$ gives the distance of the kth stimulus to each of the L centers). The second step transforms $\mathbf{d}_k$ into an $L \times 1$ similarity vector, denoted $\mathbf{s}_k$ using an elementwise function denoted $\varrho(x)$ (read "rho of x"). Several choices are possible for the ϱ functions. The most popular one is the *Gaussian* function:

$$\varrho(x) = \frac{1}{\sqrt{2\pi\sigma^2}} \exp\left\{-\frac{x^2}{2\sigma^2}\right\} , \qquad (4.19)$$

with $\exp\{x\} = \mathbf{e}^x$ being the exponential of x ($\mathbf{e} \approx 2.719$ is Euler's number, i.e., the base of natural logarithms) and σ^2 being a parameter called the *variance* of the Gaussian distribution. The variance can be specified for each center separately if necessary (i.e., σ^2_ℓ is an additional parameter). After transformation of $\mathbf{x}_k$ into $\mathbf{s}_k$, a standard heteroassociator is used to associate each pattern $\mathbf{s}_k$ to each target $\mathbf{t}_k$.

Eq. 4.18 can be rewritten in a more inclusive form using matrix notation. Denoting $\mathbf{C}$ the $L \times I$ matrix of the centers (i.e., $\mathbf{c}^T_\ell$ is the

ℓth row of $\mathbf{C}$), the distances of the K observations to the L centers can be represented by an $L \times K$ matrix $\mathbf{D}$, whose generic term $d_{\mathbf{c}_\ell, \mathbf{x}_k}$ is the Euclidean distance from observation k to center ℓ:

$$
\begin{aligned}
\mathbf{D} = [d_{\mathbf{c}_\ell, \mathbf{x}_k}] &= \left[\sqrt{(\mathbf{c}_\ell - \mathbf{x}_k)^T (\mathbf{c}_\ell - \mathbf{x}_k)} \right] \\
&= \left[\sqrt{\mathbf{c}_\ell^T \mathbf{c}_\ell + \mathbf{x}_k^T \mathbf{x}_k - 2\mathbf{c}_\ell^T \mathbf{x}_k} \right] \\
&= \sqrt{(\mathbf{C} \circledast \mathbf{C}) \times {}_I \mathbf{1}_K + {}_L \mathbf{1}_I \times (\mathbf{X} \circledast \mathbf{X}) - 2 \times \mathbf{C} \times \mathbf{X}}, \quad (4.20)
\end{aligned}
$$

with $\circledast$ denoting the elementwise (or Hadamar, see e.g., Searle, 1982) product, ${}_I\mathbf{1}_K$ being an $I \times K$ matrix of 1's, the square root function being applied elementwise to the matrix, and $\mathbf{X}$ being the $I \times K$ matrix of the K input patterns applied to the I input cells. The $L \times K$ distance matrix is then transformed into an $L \times K$ similarity matrix denoted $\mathbf{S}$ as $\mathbf{S} = [s_{\ell,k}] = [\varrho(d_{\mathbf{c}_\ell, \mathbf{x}_k})]$.

Then, the problem is to find an $L \times J$ matrix $\mathbf{W}$ such that $\mathbf{T} \approx \mathbf{W}^T \mathbf{S}$, with $\mathbf{T}$ being the $J \times K$ matrix of the K output patterns. If $\mathbf{S}$ is a nonsingular square matrix, the solution is given by (from Eq. 4.9 on page 58) $\mathbf{W}^T = \mathbf{T}\mathbf{S}^{-1}$. If $\mathbf{S}$ is singular or rectangular, a least squares approximation is given by (from Eq. 4.11 on page 59)

$$
\mathbf{W}^T = \mathbf{T}\mathbf{S}^+, \quad (4.21)
$$

with $\mathbf{S}^+$ being the pseudo-inverse of $\mathbf{S}$. One reason for the popularity of the Gaussian transformation is that it ensures that when $\mathbf{D}$ is a square matrix, and when the centers are not redundant (i.e., no center is present twice), then the matrix $\mathbf{S}$ is not only nonsingular but also positive definite (Michelli, 1986). Note that, even though $\mathbf{D}$ is a distance matrix, it is in general *not* full rank and not even positive semi-definite, which is the main motivation for transforming the distance to the centers into a similarity.

If the testing set is different from the learning set, then the distance from each element of the testing set to each of the centers needs to be computed. This distance is then transformed into a similarity using the ϱ function before being multiplied by the matrix $\mathbf{W}$ to give the estimation of the response to the testing set by the radial basis function network. The response of the network to a pattern $\mathbf{x}$ (old or new) is obtained by first transforming this pattern into $\mathbf{d}$ (the vector of distance from $\mathbf{x}$ to the L centers $\mathbf{c}_\ell$), then transforming $\mathbf{d}$ into a similarity vector $\mathbf{s}$, and finally obtaining the response as

$$
\widehat{\mathbf{t}} = \mathbf{W}^T \mathbf{s}. \quad (4.22)
$$

If we denote by $\mathbf{w}_\ell$ the $J \times 1$ vector storing the ℓth column of $\mathbf{W}^T$, Eq. 4.18 on page 63 can be rewritten as

$$\hat{\mathbf{t}} = \mathbf{W}^T \mathbf{s} = [\mathbf{w}_1, \ldots, \mathbf{w}_\ell, \ldots, \mathbf{w}_L]\mathbf{s} = \sum_\ell s_\ell \mathbf{w}_\ell = \sum_\ell s_\ell \phi(d_{\mathbf{c}_k, \mathbf{x}_\ell}) \; .$$
(4.23)

This shows that this variation of the linear heteroassociator implements the technique of radial basis function interpolation.

4.8.3 Radial Basis Function Networks: an Example

To illustrate a simple radial basis function network, suppose that the function to be approximated associates the following one-dimensional (i.e., $I = J = 1$) set of $K = 7$ stimuli to their response:

$$
\begin{array}{llll}
x_1 = 0 & \longmapsto & t_1 = 1 \qquad x_2 = 2 & \longmapsto \quad t_2 = 1 \\
x_3 = 3 & \longmapsto & t_3 = 2 \qquad x_4 = 4 & \longmapsto \quad t_4 = 3 \\
x_5 = 5 & \longmapsto & t_5 = 2 \qquad x_6 = 6 & \longmapsto \quad t_6 = 1 \\
x_7 = 8 & \longmapsto & t_7 = 1
\end{array}
$$

(example from Abdi, 1994b). Using matrix notation, the set of stimuli is stored in the $I \times K = 1 \times 7$ matrix $\mathbf{X}$, and the set of responses is stored in the $J \times K = 1 \times 7$ matrix $\mathbf{T}$:

$$\mathbf{X} = [0 \quad 2 \quad 3 \quad 4 \quad 5 \quad 6 \quad 8] \text{ and } \mathbf{T} = [1 \quad 1 \quad 2 \quad 3 \quad 2 \quad 1 \quad 1] \; .$$

Suppose that the set of L centers is the same as the set of inputs. It is represented by an $L \times I = 7 \times 1$ matrix:

$$\mathbf{C} = \mathbf{X}^T = [0 \quad 2 \quad 3 \quad 4 \quad 5 \quad 6 \quad 8]^T \; .$$

The matrix $\mathbf{D}$ giving the distance between the centers (represented by rows) and the stimuli (represented by columns) is equal to

$$
\mathbf{D} = \begin{bmatrix}
0 & 2 & 3 & 4 & 5 & 6 & 8 \\
2 & 0 & 1 & 2 & 3 & 4 & 6 \\
3 & 1 & 0 & 1 & 2 & 3 & 5 \\
4 & 2 & 1 & 0 & 1 & 2 & 4 \\
5 & 3 & 2 & 1 & 0 & 1 & 3 \\
6 & 4 & 3 & 2 & 1 & 0 & 2 \\
8 & 6 & 5 & 4 & 3 & 2 & 0
\end{bmatrix} \; .
$$

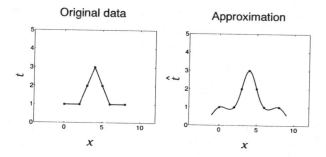

Figure 4.6: RBF approximation example: Original data and approximation.

Using the Gaussian transformation, with $\sigma^2 = 1$, the matrix $\mathbf{D}$ is then transformed into a matrix of similarities:

$$\mathbf{S} = [s_{\ell,k}] = [\varrho(d_{\mathbf{c}_\ell,\mathbf{x}_k})] = \left[\frac{1}{\sqrt{2\pi}} \exp\{-\tfrac{1}{2}d^2_{\mathbf{c}_\ell,\mathbf{x}_k}\}\right], \qquad (4.24)$$

which gives

$$\mathbf{S} = \begin{bmatrix} 0.3989 & 0.0540 & 0.0044 & 0.0001 & 0 & 0 & 0 \\ 0.0540 & 0.3989 & 0.2420 & 0.0540 & 0.0044 & 0.0001 & 0 \\ 0.0044 & 0.2420 & 0.3989 & 0.2420 & 0.0540 & 0.0044 & 0 \\ 0.0001 & 0.0540 & 0.2420 & 0.3989 & 0.2420 & 0.0540 & 0.0001 \\ 0 & 0.0044 & 0.0540 & 0.2420 & 0.3989 & 0.2420 & 0.0044 \\ 0 & 0.0001 & 0.0044 & 0.0540 & 0.2420 & 0.3989 & 0.0540 \\ 0 & 0 & 0 & 0.0001 & 0.0044 & 0.0540 & 0.3989 \end{bmatrix}.$$

The optimum matrix of weights, which would be found by a heteroassociator using Widrow-Hoff learning, can be computed by first inverting the matrix $\mathbf{S}$:

$$\mathbf{S}^{-1} = \begin{bmatrix} 2.586 & -0.634 & 0.544 & -0.352 & 0.193 & -0.076 & 0.008 \\ -0.634 & 5.074 & -4.770 & 3.183 & -1.766 & 0.702 & -0.076 \\ 0.544 & -4.770 & 9.317 & -7.408 & 4.354 & -1.766 & 0.193 \\ -0.352 & 3.183 & -7.408 & 10.631 & -7.408 & 3.183 & -0.352 \\ 0.193 & -1.766 & 4.354 & -7.408 & 9.317 & -4.770 & 0.544 \\ -0.076 & 0.702 & -1.766 & 3.183 & -4.770 & 5.074 & -0.634 \\ 0.008 & -0.076 & 0.193 & -0.352 & 0.544 & -0.634 & 2.586 \end{bmatrix}$$

and then premultiplying $\mathbf{S}^{-1}$ by $\mathbf{T}$:

$$\mathbf{W}^T = \mathbf{T}\mathbf{S}^{-1} = \begin{bmatrix} 2.302 & 1.541 & -0.679 & 7.925 & -0.679 & 1.541 & 2.302 \end{bmatrix}.$$

These weights can be used to compute the network response to a training stimulus (in this example, the training stimulus will give a response which matches the target perfectly), or they can be used to approximate a response to a stimulus not in the training set. To calculate the answer of the radial basis function network to a stimulus (old or new), it suffices to compute the distance vector from that stimulus to the seven centers, to transform it into a similarity vector using the Gaussian function, and to premultiply it by the matrix $\mathbf{W}^T$. For example, the response of the network to the new stimulus $\mathbf{x} = 1$ (where each element of $\mathbf{d}$ is the distance from $\mathbf{x}$ to the ℓth center) is

$$\hat{\mathbf{t}} = \mathbf{W}^T\mathbf{s} = \mathbf{W}^T\varrho(\mathbf{d})$$

$$= [2.30\ 1.54\ -0.68\ 7.93\ -0.68\ 1.54\ 2.30] \times \varrho\left\{\begin{bmatrix} 1 \\ 1 \\ 2 \\ 3 \\ 4 \\ 5 \\ 7 \end{bmatrix}\right\}$$

$$= [2.30\ 1.54\ -0.68\ 7.93\ -0.68\ 1.54\ 2.30] \times \begin{bmatrix} 0.242 \\ 0.242 \\ 0.054 \\ 0.004 \\ 0.000 \\ 0.000 \\ 0.000 \end{bmatrix} \approx .93. \qquad (4.25)$$

The approximation given by the radial basis function network is illustrated in Fig. 4.6 (right) for the set of input patterns belonging to the interval $[-1,\ 9]$. When compared to a straight line approximation (in Fig. 4.6, left), the network approximation appears quite smooth. Notice that the approximation for $\mathbf{x} = 1$ matches the calculation in Eq. 4.25. Note also that, as required, the approximation is perfect for the elements of the training set.

4.8.3.1 The Choice of Centers and σ's

When a radial basis function network is used for approximating a function (i.e., when the set of centers is smaller than the set of training stimuli), the choice of the centers, as well as the choice of values for σ, becomes very important. This choice, in fact, determines in part the quality of the estimation given by the network. The set of centers is sometimes learned using unsupervised learning techniques such as k-means. The variance of the ϕ function can be approximated similarly from the sample. However, in both cases, choosing centers and their variance(s) can be a very delicate operation.

5. ERROR BACKPROPAGATION

5.1 Overview

The main problem with early neural network models was that they were restricted to dealing with linear problems. Researchers (e.g., McCulloch & Pitts, 1943) knew very early that this limitation could be overcome by adding one or more hidden layers between the input and the output layers. What was missing was a perceptron-like learning rule that could be used to adjust the weights of cells of the hidden layers. This is what error backpropagation does. Its absence was probably one of the causes of the decline of interest in neural networks at the end of the 1960s, and its emergence contributed to the "revival" of the 1980s. This algorithm was (re)discovered several times since the 1950s but gained acceptance in the mid-1980s (see, e.g., Rojas, 1996, p. 180*ff.*, for a historical sketch). It adjusts the weights in any feedforward network trained to associate pairs of patterns.

Backpropagation networks are multilayer networks made of nonlinear units.[1] Like a linear unit, a nonlinear unit computes its activation level by summing all the weighted activations it receives. However, unlike a linear unit, a nonlinear unit transforms its activation into a response via a nonlinear transfer function. The goal of backpropagation networks is to learn nonlinear mappings between pairs of input-output patterns. These networks can be used as pattern classifiers or more generally to solve nonlinear problems. They can also be used as a tool for exploring knowledge representation (e.g., in psychology). In this case, the hidden layer acts as the internal representation.

A backpropagation network is similar to a perceptron and a linear heteroassociator in some ways and differs in other ways. Like a perceptron and a linear heteroassociator, a backpropagation network uses supervised learning: The difference between the response of an output unit and the expected response is the error made by the network. This serves as a basis for connection weight correction. The cells of the output layer use this error directly to correct their connecting weights in a manner akin to the cells of a linear heteroassociator.

---

[1] Actually, only the hidden cells need to be nonlinear.

The cells of the hidden layer are not in direct contact with the error. They need to *estimate* their error. To do so they use *error backpropagation*. The amount of error made by the network is first converted into an *error signal* that is proportional to the rate of change (i.e., slope or derivative) of the nonlinear transfer function. This error signal is then passed backward (backpropagated) through the connection weights to the hidden units. The hidden units estimate their error as a *weighted sum of the error signals received from the connected output units*. If an output unit has a large error, or if the weight between the hidden unit and the output unit is large, then the error signal for the hidden unit will be large. After the error signal of the hidden units has been estimated, all connection weights are updated in proportion to their error signal. To recap: The new notions for backpropagation are as follows:

> (1) multiple layers of nonlinear units, (2) computation of an error signal using the rate of change of the nonlinear function, (3) backpropagation of an error signal, and (4) estimation of an error signal by the hidden units.

5.2 Architecture and Notation

A backpropagation network is made of three different types of layers: one input layer, one (or several) hidden layer(s), and one output layer (see Fig. 5.1 on the next page). For simplicity, in what follows we will consider only the case of single hidden layer networks, but all the notions presented can be easily generalized to more complex networks.

The kth stimulus described by I features is represented as an $I \times 1$ vector $\mathbf{x}_k$. The response of the hidden units for the kth stimulus is represented by an $L \times 1$ vector $\mathbf{h}_k$, where L represents the number of hidden units. The response of the output units for the kth stimulus is represented by a $J \times 1$ vector $\widehat{\mathbf{t}}_k$, where J represents the number of output units. The desired output for the kth stimulus is represented by a $J \times 1$ vector $\mathbf{t}_k$. The intensities of the connections between the input units and the hidden units is given by an $I \times L$ matrix $\mathbf{Z}$. The intensities of the connections between the hidden units and the output units is given by an $L \times J$ matrix $\mathbf{W}$. It is necessary for matrix $\mathbf{W}$ to be "initialized" with (i.e., to have starting values set as) nonzero numbers (see note 5 on page 73). The standard practice is to initialize matrices $\mathbf{Z}$ and $\mathbf{W}$ with small random numbers. The hidden units perform a nonlinear mapping of the input layer onto the output

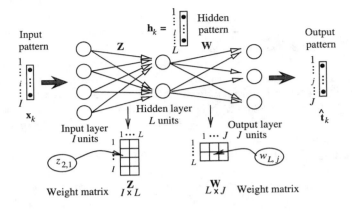

Figure 5.1: A three-layer backpropagation network.

layer. This mapping is done via a "transfer function" denoted $f(x)$ applied to their activation level. Learning results from the modification of the values of the two sets of connections. These modifications are implemented with error backpropagation.

5.3 The Building Block: The Nonlinear Unit

Each unit of a backpropagation network layer is connected to all the units of the preceding and following layers. The units within the hidden and output layers are *nonlinear* (but see note 1 on page 68). Like the linear unit, the nonlinear unit computes its activation level by adding all the weighted activations it receives (as given by Eqs. 3.1 and 3.2, page 23; see Fig. 5.2 on the facing page). However, unlike the linear unit, it will transform this activation[2] level into a response using a *nonlinear transfer function*. Several transfer functions can be used. The most popular one is the *logistic function*:

$$f(x) = \text{logist}(x) = \frac{1}{1 + \exp\{-x\}}. \tag{5.1}$$

---

[2]If a threshold is used, then its value is subtracted from the activation before transformation. Equivalently, an extra cell for each layer can be clamped to the value -1 (or $+1$) so that the weight of its connection with each cell is the threshold (or the negative threshold) of the cell (*cf.* Eq. 2.3 on page 5).

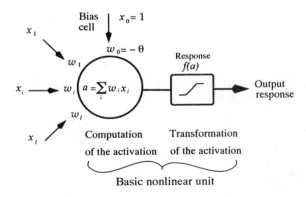

Basic nonlinear unit

Figure 5.2: A basic nonlinear unit computes its activation as a weighted sum of its inputs and transforms it into a response with a nonlinear transfer function.

This function maps the set of real numbers into the $[0, 1]$ range. It has the attractive property of having a derivative easy to compute:

$$f'(x) = \frac{d \, \text{logist}(x)}{dx} = \text{logist}(x) \, [1 - \text{logist}(x)] = f(x)[1 - f(x)]. \tag{5.2}$$

The hyperbolic tangent is also often used when the response range is the interval $[-1, +1]$:

$$f(x) = \tanh(x) = \frac{\exp\{x\} - \exp\{-x\}}{\exp\{x\} + \exp\{-x\}} = 2 \times \text{logist}(2x) - 1 \,. \tag{5.3}$$

It is, in fact, simply a rescaling of the logistic function adjusted to the $[-1, +1]$ range. Its derivative is also easy to compute:

$$f'(x) = \frac{d \tanh(x)}{dx} = \frac{4}{(\exp\{x\} + \exp\{-x\})^2} \,. \tag{5.4}$$

These two transfer functions and their derivatives are shown in Fig. 5.3 on the following page. Each layer may have a different number of units and a different transfer function. In this chapter we will present the simplest case of a single logistic transfer function.

5.3.1 What's New in a Nonlinear Unit: Using the Derivative

Linear and nonlinear units learn, when using the Widrow-Hoff learning rule, by correcting their connection weights iteratively. For a linear unit, the correction is proportional to the error made and to the

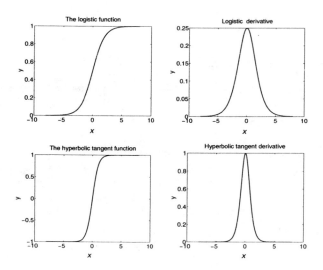

Figure 5.3: Two nonlinear transfer functions and their derivatives.

value of the input cell (see Eq. 3.15 on page 38). For a nonlinear unit, we need to add another constraint: The intensity of the correction should be small when the output of the cell is near its asymptotic values (e.g., 0 and 1 for the logistic), and the correction should be large when the output of the cell is in the middle of its range (e.g., .5 for a logistic). In fact, we want the correction to be proportional to the *rate of change* of the transfer function. The easiest way[3] to fulfill this requirement is to make the correction proportional to the *derivative* of the transfer function. This works because, as shown in Fig. 5.3, the derivative of a sigmoid function has the shape of a bell. It reaches its highest value when the sigmoid is in the middle of its range and tends toward zero when the sigmoid tends toward its asymptotes. To recap: The correction to be applied during Widrow-Hoff learning for the weight of a nonlinear unit is proportional to (1) the derivative of the transfer function of the activation of this unit, (2) the amount of the error made, and (3) the activation of the input cell. Formally, the correction applied at a given time to the weight $w_{\ell,j}$ connecting hidden cell ℓ to output cell j is equal to

$$\Delta_{w_{\ell,j}} = f'(a_j) \times (t_j - \widehat{t_j}) \times h_\ell, \tag{5.5}$$

with $f'(a_j)$ the value of the derivative of the transfer function applied to the value of the activation of cell j, t_j the target value for

---

[3]When one remembers one's calculus, that is!

cell j, $\hat{t}_j$ the response of cell j [therefore $e_j = (t_j - \hat{t}_j)$, called the *error term*, is the error made by cell j], and h_ℓ the value transmitted from cell ℓ. The term $f'(a_j) \times (t_j - \hat{t}_j)$ is called the *error signal* and is denoted δ_j for cell j (note that it is different from the error term). Eq. 5.5 can, therefore, be rewritten in a more compact way as[4]

$$\Delta_{w_{\ell,j}} = [f'(a_j) \times e_j] \times h_\ell = \delta_j \times h_\ell$$
$$= \text{(error signal for cell } j) \times \text{(activation of cell } \ell). \qquad (5.6)$$

(Note, by the way, that a linear unit uses, in fact, the same updating rule because the derivative of a linear function is a constant.) For a cell of the hidden layer, the error term $(t - \hat{t})$ is not available (because only the cells of the output layer have a target value). The error term of the hidden cell is estimated as the *weighted sum* of the error signals of the output layer cells (i.e., the error signal of each output cell is weighted by its connection from the hidden cell). Formally, the estimation of the error term of hidden cell ℓ, noted $\hat{e}_\ell$, is computed as

$$\hat{e}_\ell = \text{weighted sum of output cell error signals} = \sum_j w_{\ell,j} \delta_j . \quad (5.7)$$

Once the error term has been estimated, the correction for a weight from input cell i to hidden cell ℓ is the same as for an output layer cell with the estimation of the error term replacing the error term:[5]

$$\Delta_{z_{i,\ell}} = [f'(a_\ell) \times \hat{e}_\ell] \times x_i = \delta_\ell \times x_i$$
$$= \text{(error signal for cell } \ell) \times \text{(activation of cell } i) . \qquad (5.8)$$

5.4 The Backpropagation Algorithm

5.4.1 Algorithm Description

The rule used for backpropagating the error is a generalization of the Delta or Widrow-Hoff learning rule. It can be used in batch mode or single stimulus mode. We present here the single stimulus mode (the batch mode equations are obtained by replacing, in the following

---

[4]Note that the output layer behaves like a heteroassociator. In particular, if the output cell transfer function is linear, the output layer is, as far as learning is concerned, a standard linear heteroassociator.

[5]Note that an error term equal to zero implies no learning. This can happen if all the w weights are zero. Therefore, initializing these weights as zero will make learning impossible. This explains the practice of using small random numbers as starting values.

equations, the terms with a k-subscript by the corresponding matrices, e.g., replace $\mathbf{t}_k$ by $\mathbf{T}$).

The backpropagation algorithm involves two phases. In the first phase, a forward flow of activation is generated from the input layer to the output layer via the hidden layer. Each unit in the hidden layer computes its activation as a weighted sum of its inputs and transforms it into its response using its transfer function. The $L \times 1$ vector of the hidden cell responses is obtained as

$$\mathbf{h}_k = f(\mathbf{Z}^T\mathbf{x}_k) \, . \tag{5.9}$$

The response of the hidden layer is the input of the output layer. The response vector of the output units is given by $\widehat{\mathbf{t}}_k = f(\mathbf{W}^T\mathbf{h}_k)$.

In the second phase, the error term, defined as the difference between the actual output and the desired output, is computed. The output cell error term vector is $\mathbf{e}_k = (\mathbf{t}_k - \widehat{\mathbf{t}}_k)$. The error term is then transformed into an error signal which takes into account the derivative of the cell activations. The error signal vector, denoted $\delta_{\text{output},k}$, for the output layer is given by (rewriting Eq. 5.5 in matrix notation)

$$\delta_{\text{output},k} = f'(\mathbf{W}^T\mathbf{h}_k) \circledast (\mathbf{e}_k) = f'(\mathbf{W}^T\mathbf{h}_k) \circledast (\mathbf{t}_k - \widehat{\mathbf{t}}_k), \tag{5.10}$$

where f' represents the derivative of the transfer function f and $\circledast$ the elementwise product of the vectors. When f is the logistic function, (see Eq. 5.2), Eq. 5.10 reduces to $\delta_{\text{output},k} = \widehat{\mathbf{t}}_k \circledast (1 - \widehat{\mathbf{t}}_k) \circledast (\mathbf{t}_k - \widehat{\mathbf{t}}_k)$, where $\mathbf{1}$ is a unit vector of the same dimensions as $\mathbf{t}_k$ (i.e., a $J \times 1$ vector whose elements are 1's).

The error signal is then backpropagated through the network, layer by layer. After the connection weights have been used to backpropagate the error, they are adjusted so as to minimize the mean-square error between the network output and the desired output. For the output layer cells, the error signal is used directly in a manner similar to the Widrow-Hoff learning rule described for the linear associators (*cf.* Eq. 3.15 on page 38 and Eq. 4.5 on page 55). The weights in the matrix $\mathbf{W}$ are changed iteratively. For the next iteration the matrix is computed as

$$\mathbf{W}_{[n+1]} = \mathbf{W}_{[n]} + \eta\mathbf{h}_k\delta_{\text{output},k}^T = \mathbf{W}_{[n]} + \Delta_{\mathbf{W}_{[n]}}, \tag{5.11}$$

where η is a small learning constant and k is randomly chosen.

The adjustment of the weights between the input units and the hidden units (i.e., the weights in matrix $\mathbf{Z}$) is proportional to both the (estimated) error $(\widehat{\mathbf{e}}_k = \mathbf{W}_{[n]}\delta_{\text{output},k}$ for stimulus k) of each hidden unit and the extent to which each specific input unit contributed to this error. The (estimated) error signal vector for the hidden units is denoted $\delta_{\text{hidden},k}$ and is obtained as a weighted combination of the output cell error signals multiplied by the derivative of the hidden cell activations. Rewriting Eqs. 5.7 and 5.8 in matrix notation gives

$$\delta_{\text{hidden},k} = f'(\mathbf{Z}^T\mathbf{x}_k) \circledast \widehat{\mathbf{e}}_k = f'(\mathbf{Z}^T\mathbf{x}_k) \circledast (\mathbf{W}_{[n]}\delta_{\text{output},k}). \quad (5.12)$$

With the logistic function, Eq. 5.12 reduces to $\delta_{\text{hidden},k} = \mathbf{h}_k \circledast (1 - \mathbf{h}_k) \circledast (\mathbf{W}_{[n]}\delta_{\text{output},k})$. Learning at iteration $n + 1$, for the cells of the hidden layer, is implemented as

$$\mathbf{Z}_{[n+1]} = \mathbf{Z}_{[n]} + \eta\mathbf{x}_k\delta^T_{\text{hidden},k} = \mathbf{Z}_{[n]} + \Delta\mathbf{z}_{[n]} . \quad (5.13)$$

We first use a small example to illustrate this algorithm, and later we will show that it is equivalent to searching for a set of values for the weights (z and w) that makes the responses of the network as close as possible (in a mean square sense) to the target values.

5.4.2 A Numerical Example

To illustrate the algorithm described in the previous section, we will use a simple numerical example: A three-layer network made of $I = 3$ input units, $L = 2$ hidden units, and $J = 3$ output units (see Fig. 5.4) will be trained to associate the stimulus $\mathbf{x} = \begin{bmatrix} 1 & 2 & 3 \end{bmatrix}^T$ to the response $\mathbf{t} = \begin{bmatrix} .1 & .3 & .7 \end{bmatrix}^T$. To keep the example simple, the cells do not use a threshold.

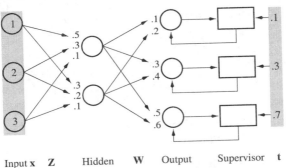

Input x   **Z**   Hidden   **W**   Output   Supervisor   **t**

Figure 5.4: Network architecture of the example. The input values, output targets, and connection weights are indicated on the figure.

The weight matrix $\mathbf{Z}$ connecting the input layer to the hidden layer is an $I \times L = 3 \times 2$ matrix (to simplify the notation, $\mathbf{Z}$ is

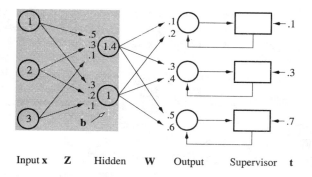

Input **x**   **Z**   Hidden   **W**   Output   Supervisor   **t**

Figure 5.5: First step of the backpropagation algorithm. The stimulus **x** = $[1\ 2\ 3]^T$ is presented to the input units which propagate their activation to the hidden units via the first set of connections. Each hidden unit computes its activation **b** as the weighted sum of its inputs.

used throughout this example instead of $\mathbf{Z}_{[n]}$). The weight matrix **W** connecting the hidden layer to the output layer is an $L \times J = 2 \times 3$ matrix (to simplify, the notation **W** is used throughout this example instead of $\mathbf{W}_{[n]}$). These matrices are equal to

$$\mathbf{Z} = \begin{bmatrix} .5 & .3 \\ .3 & .2 \\ .1 & .1 \end{bmatrix} , \qquad \mathbf{W} = \begin{bmatrix} .1 & .3 & .5 \\ .2 & .4 & .6 \end{bmatrix} . \tag{5.14}$$

The algorithm starts by forwarding the input activation to the output units via the hidden units. First, the hidden units compute their level of activation (see Fig. 5.5), denoted **b**, as

$$\mathbf{b} = \mathbf{Z}^T \mathbf{x} = \begin{bmatrix} .5 & .3 & .1 \\ .3 & .2 & .1 \end{bmatrix} \times \begin{bmatrix} 1 \\ 2 \\ 3 \end{bmatrix} = \begin{bmatrix} 1.4 \\ 1.0 \end{bmatrix} . \tag{5.15}$$

Next, this activation is transformed into a response by using the logistic function (see Fig. 5.6):

$$\mathbf{h} = f(\mathbf{b}) = f\left(\begin{bmatrix} 1.4 \\ 1.0 \end{bmatrix}\right) = \begin{bmatrix} \dfrac{1}{1 + \exp\{-1.4\}} \\ \dfrac{1}{1 + \exp\{-1.0\}} \end{bmatrix} = \begin{bmatrix} 0.8022 \\ 0.7311 \end{bmatrix} .$$

This response is then forwarded to the output units, which com-

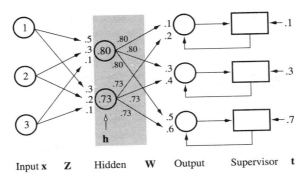

Figure 5.6: The hidden units transform their activation into a response **h** using the logistic function. The response is then propagated to the output units via the second set of connections.

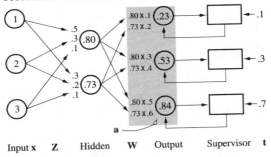

Figure 5.7: The output units compute their activation **a** as the weighted sum of their input.

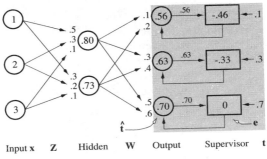

Figure 5.8: The output units transform their activation into a response $\hat{\mathbf{t}}$ via the logistic function and propagate it to the supervisor, which computes the error, $\mathbf{e} = \mathbf{t} - \hat{\mathbf{t}}$.

pute their activation (see Fig. 5.7),

$$\mathbf{a} = \mathbf{W}^T\mathbf{h} = \begin{bmatrix} .1 & .2 \\ .3 & .4 \\ .5 & .6 \end{bmatrix} \times \begin{bmatrix} .8022 \\ .7311 \end{bmatrix} = \begin{bmatrix} 0.2264 \\ 0.5331 \\ 0.8397 \end{bmatrix}, \qquad (5.16)$$

and transform it into a response, using the logistic function (Fig. 5.8):

$$\widehat{\mathbf{t}} = f(\mathbf{a}) = f\left(\begin{bmatrix} .2264 \\ .5331 \\ .8397 \end{bmatrix}\right) = \begin{bmatrix} \dfrac{1}{1 + \exp\{-.2264\}} \\[2mm] \dfrac{1}{1 + \exp\{-.5331\}} \\[2mm] \dfrac{1}{1 + \exp\{-.8397\}} \end{bmatrix} = \begin{bmatrix} 0.5564 \\ 0.6302 \\ 0.6984 \end{bmatrix}.$$

The first step is now accomplished, and learning can begin. The error is computed by the "supervisor" as the difference between the computed response $\widehat{\mathbf{t}}$ and the expected response $\mathbf{t}$ (see Fig. 5.8):

$$\mathbf{e} = \mathbf{t} - \widehat{\mathbf{t}} = \begin{bmatrix} .1 \\ .3 \\ .7 \end{bmatrix} - \begin{bmatrix} 0.5564 \\ 0.6302 \\ 0.6984 \end{bmatrix} = \begin{bmatrix} -0.4564 \\ -0.3302 \\ 0.0016 \end{bmatrix}. \qquad (5.17)$$

To compute the error signal δ_{output}, the first step is to compute the derivative of the output unit responses:

$$f'(\mathbf{a}) = \widehat{\mathbf{t}} \circledast (1 - \widehat{\mathbf{t}}) = \begin{bmatrix} 0.5564 \\ 0.6302 \\ 0.6984 \end{bmatrix} \circledast \left(\begin{bmatrix} 1 \\ 1 \\ 1 \end{bmatrix} - \begin{bmatrix} 0.5564 \\ 0.6302 \\ 0.6984 \end{bmatrix}\right)$$

$$= \begin{bmatrix} 0.5564 \\ 0.6302 \\ 0.6984 \end{bmatrix} \circledast \begin{bmatrix} 0.4436 \\ 0.3698 \\ 0.3016 \end{bmatrix} = \begin{bmatrix} 0.2468 \\ 0.2330 \\ 0.2106 \end{bmatrix}. \qquad (5.18)$$

The error signal is then computed as the elementwise product of this derivative and the error (see Fig. 5.9):

$$\delta_{\text{output}} = f'(\mathbf{a}) \circledast \mathbf{e} = \widehat{\mathbf{t}} \circledast (1 - \widehat{\mathbf{t}}) \circledast (\mathbf{t} - \widehat{\mathbf{t}})$$

$$= \begin{bmatrix} 0.2468 \\ 0.2330 \\ 0.2106 \end{bmatrix} \circledast \begin{bmatrix} -0.4564 \\ -0.3302 \\ 0.0016 \end{bmatrix} = \begin{bmatrix} -0.1126 \\ -0.0770 \\ 0.0003 \end{bmatrix}. \qquad (5.19)$$

The output units will now backpropagate this error signal to the hidden units. First, the amount of output error attributable to each

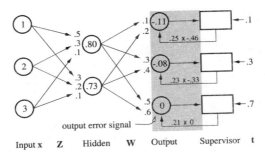

Figure 5.9: The output units compute their error signal $\delta_{\text{output}} = f'(a) \circledast e$.

hidden unit is estimated by multiplying the error signal of each output unit by the weights in $\mathbf{W}$, which connect the hidden layer to the output layer. This propagation of the output error signal is illustrated in Fig. 5.10. Each hidden unit then sums its estimated error received

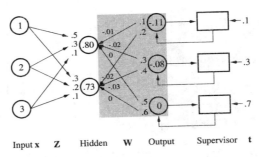

Figure 5.10: The output units propagate the error signal to the hidden units: The error signal is first multiplied by the connection weights between output and hidden units and then sent to the hidden units.

from this backpropagation (see Fig. 5.11). Formally, this estimation of hidden unit "responsibility" for output error is computed by a matrix multiplication, which gives the estimate of the hidden unit error term vector, denoted $\widehat{e}$, as

$$\widehat{e} = \mathbf{W}\delta_{\text{output}} = \begin{bmatrix} .1 & .3 & .5 \\ .2 & .4 & .6 \end{bmatrix} \times \begin{bmatrix} -0.1126 \\ -0.0770 \\ 0.0003 \end{bmatrix} = \begin{bmatrix} -0.0342 \\ -0.0531 \end{bmatrix}.$$

The error signal of the hidden units is then computed similarly to the error signal of the output units, except that the error given by the supervisor is replaced by the estimation of the hidden layer error.

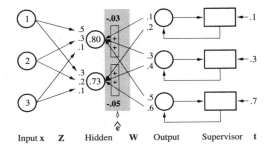

Figure 5.11: Each hidden unit computes the sum of the error signal it receives. This amounts to computing the vector $\hat{\mathbf{e}}$.

First, the derivative of the hidden unit responses is computed:

$$f'(\mathbf{b}) = \mathbf{h} \circledast (1 - \mathbf{h}) = \begin{bmatrix} 0.8022 \\ 0.7311 \end{bmatrix} \circledast \left(\begin{bmatrix} 1 \\ 1 \end{bmatrix} - \begin{bmatrix} 0.8022 \\ 0.7311 \end{bmatrix} \right)$$

$$= \begin{bmatrix} 0.8022 \\ 0.7311 \end{bmatrix} \circledast \begin{bmatrix} 0.1978 \\ 0.2689 \end{bmatrix} = \begin{bmatrix} 0.1587 \\ 0.1966 \end{bmatrix} \tag{5.20}$$

and then the error signal is given by

$$\delta_{\text{hidden}} = f'(\mathbf{b}) \circledast \hat{\mathbf{e}} = \mathbf{h} \circledast (1 - \mathbf{h}) \circledast (\mathbf{W}\delta_{\text{output}})$$

$$= \begin{bmatrix} 0.1587 \\ 0.1966 \end{bmatrix} \circledast \begin{bmatrix} -0.0342 \\ -0.0531 \end{bmatrix} = \begin{bmatrix} -0.0054 \\ -0.0104 \end{bmatrix}. \tag{5.21}$$

Fig. 5.12 illustrates this computation of the hidden unit error signal.

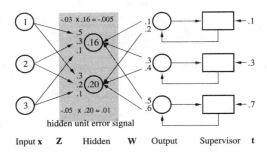

Figure 5.12: The hidden units compute their error signal $\delta_{\text{hidden}} = f'(\mathbf{b}) \circledast \hat{\mathbf{e}} = \mathbf{h} \circledast (1 - \mathbf{h}) \circledast (\mathbf{W}\delta_{\text{output}})$.

Once the error signal is backpropagated to the hidden layer (through the weight matrix $\mathbf{W}$), the synaptic weights are corrected.

Fig. 5.13 and Fig. 5.14 illustrate the steps to correct the weight matrix between the units of the input and hidden layers. The weight matrix $\mathbf{Z}$ can be corrected as $\mathbf{Z}_{[n+1]}$:

$$\mathbf{Z}_{[n+1]} = \mathbf{Z} + \boldsymbol{\Delta}_{\mathbf{Z}} = \mathbf{Z} + \eta \mathbf{x} \boldsymbol{\delta}^T_{\text{hidden}}$$

$$= \begin{bmatrix} .5 & .3 \\ .3 & .2 \\ .1 & .1 \end{bmatrix} + 1 \times \left(\begin{bmatrix} 1 \\ 2 \\ 3 \end{bmatrix} \times [-0.0054 \quad -0.0104] \right)$$

$$= \begin{bmatrix} .5 & .3 \\ .3 & .2 \\ .1 & .1 \end{bmatrix} + \begin{bmatrix} -0.0054 & -0.0104 \\ -0.0108 & -0.0209 \\ -0.0163 & -0.0313 \end{bmatrix}$$

$$= \begin{bmatrix} .4946 & .2896 \\ .2892 & .1791 \\ .0837 & .0687 \end{bmatrix} . \tag{5.22}$$

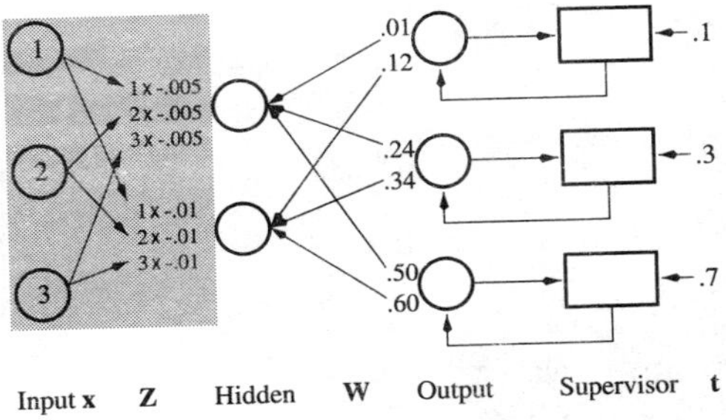

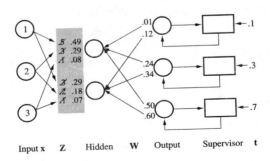

Figure 5.13: The hidden units compute the corrections to apply to the connection matrix $\mathbf{Z}$, $\boldsymbol{\Delta}_{\mathbf{Z}} = \eta \mathbf{x} \boldsymbol{\delta}^T_{\text{hidden}}$ with $\eta = 1$.

Figure 5.14: The hidden units update the weight matrix: $\mathbf{Z}_{[n+1]} = \mathbf{Z} + \boldsymbol{\Delta}_{\mathbf{Z}}$.

82

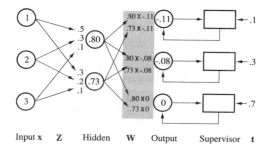

Figure 5.15: The output units compute the correction $\Delta\mathbf{w}$.

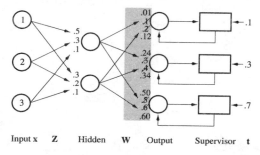

Figure 5.16: The output units update $\mathbf{W}$: $\mathbf{W}_{[n+1]} = \mathbf{W} + \Delta\mathbf{w}$, and a new iteration can begin.

Each output unit also corrects its synaptic weights. This is done by computing $\Delta\mathbf{w}$ (see Fig. 5.15):

$$\Delta\mathbf{w} = \eta\mathbf{h}\boldsymbol{\delta}_{\text{output}}^T = 1 \times \begin{bmatrix} 0.8022 \\ 0.7311 \end{bmatrix} \begin{bmatrix} -0.1126 & -0.0770 & 0.0003 \end{bmatrix}$$

$$= \begin{bmatrix} -0.0904 & -0.0617 & 0.0003 \\ -0.0823 & -0.0563 & 0.0002 \end{bmatrix} \tag{5.23}$$

and updating $\mathbf{W}$ (see Fig. 5.16), which becomes

$$\mathbf{W}_{[n+1]} = \mathbf{W} + \Delta\mathbf{w} = \begin{bmatrix} .1 & .3 & .5 \\ .2 & .4 & .6 \end{bmatrix} + \begin{bmatrix} -0.0904 & -0.0617 & 0.0003 \\ -0.0823 & -0.0563 & 0.0002 \end{bmatrix}$$

$$= \begin{bmatrix} 0.0096 & 0.2383 & 0.5003 \\ 0.1177 & 0.3437 & 0.6002 \end{bmatrix}. \tag{5.24}$$

Et voilà! These steps are repeated, using the corrected weight matrices, until the output responses are perfect (i.e., match the target values) or until some other criterion is met.

5.5 Performance Analysis

5.5.1 XOR: *The Revenge*

The XOR logical function (which the perceptron cannot learn because it is nonlinear) is traditionally used as a test for neural networks. In this section, we show that a backpropagation network can learn this function. The first difficulty in training a backpropagation network to solve the XOR problem is that a logical function is a binary function (i.e., it takes on exact values: 1 and 0). Because the 0 and 1 values are asymptotes of the logistic function, the activation of the output cell would have to reach infinity for the solution to be found, which is clearly impossible. To eliminate this problem, the 0 and 1 values are replaced by some reachable values such as .1 and .9. Then the problem becomes that of associating the following pairs of stimuli:

$$\mathbf{x}_1 = [0 \quad 0]^T \longrightarrow t_1 = .1, \qquad \mathbf{x}_2 = [1 \quad 0]^T \longrightarrow t_2 = .9$$

$$\mathbf{x}_3 = [0 \quad 1]^T \longrightarrow t_3 = .9, \qquad \mathbf{x}_4 = [1 \quad 1]^T \longrightarrow t_4 = .1$$

The next step is to choose the architecture of the network. Here we decided to use a network with two input units, three hidden units, and one output unit (the hidden cells and the output cell have a nonzero threshold). We first initialize the weight matrices $\mathbf{Z}$ and $\mathbf{W}$ with small random values. Then we apply the backpropagation algorithm presented in the previous section with a learning constant of $\eta = .45$. After each epoch, the performance of the network is evaluated by computing an error sum of squares (*cf.* Section 3.8 on page 36). After some 5,000 epochs of learning, the network finds the following values for the weight matrices. This implements the XOR function:

$$\mathbf{Z} = \begin{bmatrix} 5.7 & 6.2 & 0.5 \\ -3.2 & 5.8 & 4.7 \end{bmatrix} \text{ and } \mathbf{W}^T = [-6.2 \quad 9.0 \quad -6.8] . \quad (5.25)$$

With threshold values of $[-1.2, 1.9, 3.0]$ for the cells of the hidden layers and $[0.6]$ for the output layer cell, the network gives (rounded to two decimal places) the following responses for each of the four stimuli: $[.03, .94, .95, .07]$, which are close enough to the target values of $[.1, .9, .9, .1]$.

The results of a simulation with 5,000 epochs are shown in Fig. 5.17 on the next page. Clearly, a large number of epochs is necessary to reach the correct solution. For about 1,000 epochs, the performance does not improve much. Using a landscape metaphor, we say that

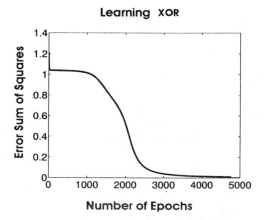

Figure 5.17: Learning the XOR function with backpropagation.

the network is "stuck" on a plateau of the error function. Then the performance improves until the network finds a set of weights corresponding to a solution of the XOR problem. We say that the network has found a valley and followed it down until a minimum of the error function is reached.

5.5.2 Pros and Cons

The XOR example shows that the first problem of a backpropagation network is the need for a very large number of iterations to reach a solution. The performance of backpropagation can be greatly improved, however, by using several techniques such as the momentum method (see, e.g., Chauvin & Rumelhart, 1995). A second problem of backpropagation networks is that finding a solution is not guaranteed, even when it exists. The minimum reached by the network might not be the bottom of the valley (or global minimum) but rather an inflection in the slope (or local minimum) after which the function goes down toward another minimum. If the network is trapped in such a minimum, learning will stop before the correct solution is reached.

Despite its shortcomings, backpropagation is probably the most popular technique used to train neural networks. One of the reasons comes from the fact that, adapting a result from Kolmogorov (see, e.g., Haykin, 1998, for more details), several authors showed in the late 1980s that backpropagation networks are universal approximators. This means that any arbitrary mapping between input and output can be implemented. However, finding the correct architecture (i.e., number of hidden layers and number of cells per layer) is still a topic for active research. When backpropagation is used with target vectors being class indicators (i.e., the jth class corresponds to a value of 1, all the other values being equal to 0), then the jth element of the response vector is an approximation of the *a posteriori* class probability (i.e., the probability that the input vector belongs to a class, given its value and the learning history).

5.6 Backpropagation and Gradient Descent

In the previous section we saw that the performance of a backpropagation network can be described in terms of the landscape of the error function. In this context, the goal of the backpropagation algorithm is to search iteratively for the minimum of the error function, using the gradient descent method described in Section 3.11 on page 45.

For an error backpropagation network, the function to minimize is the error function defined as the sum of squares of the differences between the expected values $\mathbf{t}_k$ and the responses of the network $\widehat{\mathbf{t}}_k$. Specifically, the error function for the kth response is given by

$$\mathcal{J}_k = \tfrac{1}{2}(\mathbf{t}_k - \widehat{\mathbf{t}}_k)^T(\mathbf{t}_k - \widehat{\mathbf{t}}_k) = \tfrac{1}{2}(\mathbf{t}_k^T\mathbf{t}_k + \widehat{\mathbf{t}}_k^T\widehat{\mathbf{t}}_k - 2\mathbf{t}_k^T\widehat{\mathbf{t}}_k) . \quad (5.26)$$

5.6.1 Correction for the Output Layer

For the output layer, the matrix of parameters is the weight matrix $\mathbf{W}$. The gradient of $\mathcal{J}_k$ relative to $\mathbf{W}$ is computed using the chain rule adapted to matrices $\nabla_{\mathbf{W}}\mathcal{J}_k = \dfrac{\partial \mathcal{J}_k}{\partial \mathbf{W}} = \dfrac{\partial \mathcal{J}_k}{\partial \widehat{\mathbf{t}}_k} \dfrac{\partial \widehat{\mathbf{t}}_k}{\partial \mathbf{W}^T\mathbf{h}_k} \dfrac{\partial \mathbf{W}^T\mathbf{h}_k}{\partial \mathbf{W}}$,

with

$$\frac{\partial \mathcal{J}_k}{\partial \widehat{\mathbf{t}}_k} = -(\mathbf{t}_k - \widehat{\mathbf{t}}_k) \quad (5.27)$$

$$\frac{\partial \widehat{\mathbf{t}}_k}{\partial \mathbf{W}^T\mathbf{h}_k} = \frac{\partial f(\mathbf{W}^T\mathbf{h}_k)}{\partial \mathbf{W}\mathbf{h}_k} = f'(\mathbf{W}^T\mathbf{h}_k) = \widehat{\mathbf{t}}_k \circledast (1 - \widehat{\mathbf{t}}_k) \quad (5.28)$$

(the term after the last equals sign is obtained assuming that f is the logistic function). And, finally, $\dfrac{\partial \mathbf{W}^T\mathbf{h}_k}{\partial \mathbf{W}} = 2\mathbf{h}_k^T$. Therefore, the correction for $\mathbf{W}$ at iteration n is proportional to

$$-\nabla_{\mathbf{W}}\mathcal{J}_k = (\mathbf{t}_k - \widehat{\mathbf{t}}_k) \circledast \widehat{\mathbf{t}}_k \circledast (1 - \widehat{\mathbf{t}}_k)\mathbf{h}_k^T = \delta_{\text{output},k}\mathbf{h}_k^T . \quad (5.29)$$

With η denoting the proportionality constant, and transposing Eq. 5.29, this amounts to defining the change for $\mathbf{W}$ at iteration n as $\boldsymbol{\Delta}_{\mathbf{W}_{[n]}} = \eta \mathbf{h}_k \boldsymbol{\delta}_{\text{output},k}^T$.

5.6.2 Gradient Correction for the Hidden Layer

For the hidden layer, the matrix of parameters is the weight matrix $\mathbf{Z}$. Using the chain rule adapted to matrices [and taking into account that $\widehat{\mathbf{t}}_k = f(\mathbf{W}^T f(\mathbf{Z}^T \mathbf{x}_k))$, see, e.g., Harville, 1998] the gradient of $\mathcal{J}_k$ relative to $\mathbf{Z}$ is obtained as

$$\nabla_{\mathbf{Z}} \mathcal{J}_k = \frac{\partial \mathcal{J}_k}{\partial \mathbf{Z}} = \left(\frac{\partial \mathcal{J}_k}{\partial \widehat{\mathbf{t}}_k} \frac{\partial \widehat{\mathbf{t}}_k}{\partial \mathbf{W}^T \mathbf{h}_k} \frac{\partial \mathbf{W}^T \mathbf{h}_k}{\partial \mathbf{h}_k} \right)^T \frac{\partial \mathbf{h}_k}{\partial \mathbf{Z}^T \mathbf{x}_k} \frac{\partial \mathbf{Z}^T \mathbf{x}_k}{\partial \mathbf{Z}} .$$

$$(5.30)$$

The first two terms of Eq. 5.30 have been defined previously and correspond to $-\boldsymbol{\delta}_{\text{output},k}$. Evaluating the other terms gives

$$\frac{\partial \mathbf{W}^T \mathbf{h}_k}{\partial \mathbf{h}_k} = \mathbf{W} \tag{5.31}$$

$$\frac{\partial \mathbf{h}_k}{\partial \mathbf{Z}^T \mathbf{x}_k} = \frac{\partial f(\mathbf{Z}^T \mathbf{x}_k)}{\partial \mathbf{Z}^T \mathbf{x}_k} = f'(\mathbf{Z}^T \mathbf{x}_k) = \mathbf{h}_k \circledast (1 - \mathbf{h}_k) , \tag{5.32}$$

[finding the last term assumes that f is the logistic function].

$$\frac{\partial \mathbf{Z}^T \mathbf{x}_k}{\partial \mathbf{Z}} = 2 \mathbf{x}_k^T . \tag{5.33}$$

Therefore, the correction for $\mathbf{Z}$ at iteration n is proportional to

$$-\nabla_{\mathbf{Z}} \mathcal{J}_k = \mathbf{W} \boldsymbol{\delta}_{\text{output},k} \circledast \mathbf{h}_k \circledast (1 - \mathbf{h}_k) \mathbf{x}_k^T = \boldsymbol{\delta}_{\text{hidden},k} \mathbf{x}_k^T. \tag{5.34}$$

Denoting again by η the proportionality constant, and transposing Eq. 5.34, this amounts to defining the change for $\mathbf{Z}$ at iteration n as

$$\boldsymbol{\Delta}_{\mathbf{Z}_{[n]}} = \eta \mathbf{x}_k \boldsymbol{\delta}_{\text{hidden},k}^T . \tag{5.35}$$

Et voilà! This completes the proof and shows that error backpropagation networks implement a gradient descent technique in order to find a set of values for $\mathbf{Z}$ and $\mathbf{W}$ that gives a minimum for the sum of squares of error.

5.7 Backpropagation and Logistic Regression

Backpropagation is closely related to the statistical technique of *non-linear regression analysis*, and in particular to *logistic* regression analysis. This relationship is easier to see in the case of a backpropagation network with one hidden cell and one output cell, using the logistic function as a transfer function for the hidden cell and a linear transfer function for the output cell. In this case, the matrix $\mathbf{Z}$ is a vector noted $\mathbf{z}$, the matrix $\mathbf{W}$ becomes a scalar noted w, and the kth target and its estimation are scalars denoted t_k and $\hat{t}_k$. From Eq. 5.26 on page 85, the network minimizes the following error function:

$$\mathcal{J} = \sum_k \mathcal{J}_k = \tfrac{1}{2}\sum_k (t_k - \hat{t}_k)^2 = \tfrac{1}{2}\sum_k \left[t_k - w\, \text{logist}(\mathbf{z}^T\mathbf{x}_k) \right]^2. \tag{5.36}$$

The logistic regression approximates this expression by using the inverse logistic function (called the *logit* function), which is defined as $\text{logit}(x) = \text{logist}^{-1}(x) = \ln(x) - \ln(1-x)$ [with $\ln(x)$ being the natural logarithm of x]. As a consequence, logistic regression finds a vector $\mathbf{v}$ that minimizes the following error function:

$$\mathcal{J}_{\text{logit}} = \tfrac{1}{2}\sum_k \left[\text{logit}(t_k) - \text{logit}(\hat{t}_k) \right]^2 = \tfrac{1}{2}\sum_k \left[\text{logit}(t_k) - w(\mathbf{v}^T\mathbf{x}_k) \right]^2. \tag{5.37}$$

This can be obtained using linear regression techniques (i.e., pseudo-inverse) and shows the close relationship between these techniques.

6. USEFUL REFERENCES

Neural network theory and applications are very active fields, which makes giving a complete bibliography a daunting task. We provide here a very short list of recent (1995 and beyond) or classic books which can serve as a starting point for further work. The books listed are the ones we found useful in writing this monograph. They are organized by themes. Unfortunately, there are a lot of other very good books that we cannot cite because of lack of space. There are also several discussion lists or homepages accessible on the World Wide Web; they can be found easily via a search engine (see, e.g., the discussion group comp.ai.neural-nets and the "neuroprose archive site" at `archive.cis.ohio-state.edu` in /pub/neuroprose). Software written for this book with the MATLAB language is available from the homepage of the first author (see page 90) or by anonymous `ftp` from `satie.u-bourgogne.fr` (in /pub/neural).

Classics. The best reference for finding original sources with a clear historical perspective are the books by Anderson and Rosenfeld (1988, 1998) and Anderson, Pellionitz, and Rosenfeld (1990). The book by Duda and Hart (1973) remains an outstanding reference. The two volumes of the "Parallel Distributed Processing Group" (Rumelhart & McClelland, 1986) became an instant classic. Among the recent textbooks, Hertz *et al.* (1991) is already a classic.

Introductory texts. Hagan *et al.*, (1996) give a very good general introduction and cover some of the mathematics needed. See also Gurney (1997), Patterson (1998), Rojas (1996), and Schalkoff (1997).

For cognitive scientists. Abdi (1994a), Abdi, Valentin, and Edelman (in press), Anderson (1995), Ballard (1997), Elman *et al.* (1996), McLeod, Plunkett, and Rolls (1998), and Levine (to appear) cover the domain at different depths and discuss the problems involved when using neural networks as models of cognition. Rolls and Treves (1998) give a neuroscience perspective.

For statisticians. Bishop (1995), Cherkassky and Mulier (1998), Looney (1997), Ripley (1996), and Vapnik (1999) are all excellent books with an eye toward pattern recognition.

For engineers. Haykin (1998) gives an in-depth coverage with extensions to signal processing; see also Hassoun (1995) and Luo and Unbehauen (1997). Two monographs cover extensively PCA models (Diamantaras & Kung, 1996) and variations over backpropagation (Shepherd, 1997).

For mathematicians. The book of Ellacott and Bose (1996) is a good introduction to the mathematics involved in neural modeling. Bertsekas and Tsitsiklis (1996), and Golden (1996) give a more advanced coverage.

References

ABDI, H. (1994a) *Les réseaux de neurones.* Grenoble, France: PUG.
ABDI, H. (1994b) "A neural network primer." *Journal of Biological Systems,* 2, 247–281.
ABDI, H., VALENTIN, D., & EDELMAN, B. (in press) *Neural networks for cognition.* Sunderland, MA: Sinauer.
ABDI, H., VALENTIN, D., O'TOOLE, A. J., & EDELMAN, B. (1996) "A Widrow-Hoff learning rule for a generalization of the linear autoassociator." *Journal of Mathematical Psychology,* 40, 175–182.
ANDERSON, J. A. (1995) *An introduction to neural networks.* Cambridge, MA: MIT Press.
ANDERSON, J. A., & ROSENFELD, E. (1988) *Neurocomputing.* Cambridge, MA: MIT Press.
ANDERSON, J. A., & ROSENFELD, E. (1998) *Talking nets.* Cambridge, MA: MIT Press.
ANDERSON, J. A., PELLIONITZ, A., & ROSENFELD, E. (1990) *Neurocomputing II.* Cambridge, MA: MIT Press.
BALLARD, D. H. (1997) *An introduction to natural computation.* Cambridge, MA: MIT Press.

BERTSEKAS, D. P., & TSITSIKLIS, J. N. (1996) *Neuro-dynamic programming*. Belmon, MA: Athena.

BISHOP, C. M. (1995) *Neural networks for pattern recognition*. Oxford, UK: Oxford University Press.

CHAUVIN, Y., & RUMELHART, D. E. (1995) *Backpropagation: Theory, architecture, and applications*. Hillsdale, NJ: Erlbaum.

CHERKASSKY, V., & MULIER, F. (1998) *Learning from data*. New York: Wiley.

CHONG, E. K., & ZAK, S. H. (1996) *An introduction to optimization*. New York: Wiley.

DIAMANTARAS, K. I., & KUNG, S. Y. (1996) *Principal component neural networks*. New York: Wiley.

DUDA, R. & HART, P. (1973) *Pattern classification and scenes analysis*. New York: Wiley.

ELLACOTT, S., & BOSE, D. (1996) *Neural networks: Deterministic methods of analysis*. London: ITC.

ELMAN, J. L., BATES, E. A., JOHNSON, M. H., KARMILOFF-SMITH, A., PARISI, D., & PLUNKETT, K. (1996) *Rethinking innateness: A connectionist perspective on development*. Cambridge, MA: MIT Press.

GOLDEN, R. M. (1996) *Mathematical methods for neural network analysis and design*. Cambridge, MA: MIT Press.

GURNEY, K. (1997) *An introduction to neural networks*. London: UCL.

HAGAN, M. T., DEMUTH, H. B., & BEALE, M. (1996) *Neural networks design*. Boston: PWS.

HARVILLE, D.A. (1998) *Matrix algebra from a statistician's perspective*. New York: Springer-Verlag.

HASSOUN, M. (1995) *Fundamentals of artificial neural networks*. Cambridge, MA: MIT Press.

HAYKIN, S. (1998) *Neural networks: A comprehensive foundation* (2nd ed.). New York: Prentice Hall.

HEBB, D. (1949) *The organization of behavior*. New York: Wiley.

HERTZ, J., KROGH, A., & PALMER, R. G. (1991) *Introduction to the theory of neural computation*. Reading, MA: Addison-Wesley.

KOHONEN, T. (1977) *Associative memory*. Berlin: Springer.

LEVINE, D. (to appear). *Neural and cognitive modeling* (2nd ed.). Hillsdale, NJ: Erlbaum.

LOONEY, C. G. (1997) *Pattern recognition using neural networks*. Oxford, UK: Oxford University Press.

LUO, F. L., & UNBEHAUEN, R. (1997) *Applied neural networks for signal processing*. Cambridge, MA: Cambridge University Press.

MAGNUS, J. R., & NEUDECKER, H. (1988) *Matrix differential calculus with applications in statistics and econometrics*. New York: Wiley.

MICHELLI, C. A. (1986) Interpolation of scattered data: Distance matrices and conditionally positive definite functions. *Constructive Approximations*, 2, 11–22.

MCCULLOCH, W. S., & PITTS, W. (1943) A logical calculus of the ideas immanent in nervous activity. *Bulletin of Mathematical Biophysics*, 5, 115–133.

MCLEOD, P., PLUNKETT, K., & ROLLS, E. T. (1998) *Introduction to connectionist modelling of cognitive processes*. Oxford, UK: Oxford University Press.

PATTERSON, D. W. (1998) *Artificial neural networks*. Upper Saddle River, NJ: Prentice-Hall.

RIPLEY, B.D. (1996) *Pattern recognition and neural networks*. Cambridge, MA: Cambridge University Press.

ROJAS, R. (1996) *Neural networks*. New York: Springer-Verlag.

ROLLS, E. T., & TREVES, A. (1998) *Neural networks and brain function*. Oxford, UK: Oxford University Press.

ROSENBLATT, F. (1961) *Principles of neurodynamics*. Washington, DC: Spartan Books.

RUMELHART, D., & MCCLELLAND, J. (1986) *Parallel distributed processing: Explorations in the microstructure of cognition*. Cambridge, MA: MIT Press.

SCHALKOFF, R. J. (1997) *Artificial neural networks*. New York: McGraw-Hill.

SEARLE, S. R. (1982) *Matrix algebra useful for statistics*. New York: Wiley.

SHEPHERD, A. J. (1997) *Second-order methods for neural networks*. London: Springer-Verlag.

VAPNIK, V. N. (1999) *Statistical learning theory*. New York: Wiley.

WIDROW, B., & STEARNS, S. (1985) *Adaptive signal processing*. New York: Prentice-Hall.

ABOUT THE AUTHORS

HERVÉ ABDI [e-mail: herve@utdallas.edu] received an M.S. in Psychology from the Université de Franche-Comté (France) in 1975, an M.S. (D.E.A.) in Economics from the Université de Clermond-Ferrand (France) in 1976, an M.S. (D.E.A.) in Neurology from the Université Louis Pasteur à Strasbourg (France) in 1977, and a Ph.D. in Mathematical Psychology from the Université d'Aix-en-Provence (France) in 1980. He was an assistant professor in the Université de Franche-Comté (France) in 1979, an associate professor in the Université de Bourgogne à Dijon (France) in 1983, and a full professor in the Université de Bourgogne à Dijon (France) in 1988. He is currently a full professor in the School of Human Development at the University of Texas at Dallas. He was a Fulbright visiting associate professor of Cognitive and Linguistic Sciences at Brown University and a visiting professor at the Université de Genève. His research interests include face processing and computational models of face processing, neural networks, computational and statistical models of cognitive processes (especially memory and learning), experimental design, and multivariate statistical analysis. He has published several books and papers (over one hundred) in these domains. His homepage is http://www.utdallas.edu/~herve

DOMINIQUE VALENTIN [e-mail: valentin@u-bourgogne.fr] received an M.S. in Psychology from the Université de Bourgogne à Dijon (1988) and a Ph.D. in Applied Cognition and Neuroscience from the University of Texas at Dallas in 1996 (School of Human Development). The topic of her dissertation was using neural networks to model face processing. She has published several papers dealing with neural networks and modeling. She is currently an associate professor at the Université de Bourgogne à Dijon. Her homepage is http://www.u-bourgogne.fr/d.valentin

BETTY EDELMAN [e-mail: bedelman@utdallas.edu] received a master's in Applied Cognition and Neuroscience from the University of Texas at Dallas in 1993. She is currently a Ph.D. student in the School of Human Development and Communication Sciences of the University of Texas at Dallas (Program in Applied Cognition and Neuroscience). Her interests include modeling of cognitive processes using neural networks.